CW00684125

BUSES
YEARBOOK 2024

Edited by ALAN MILLAR

BUSES

YEARBOOK 2024

FRONT COVER: *Greater Manchester's new franchised Bee Network livery on Diamond North West 40810 (MX21 AUK), a Wright StreetDeck. See p6.* RUSSELL YOUNG

PREVIOUS PAGE: *A drone-mounted camera captures Souls of Olney Y5 BUS, a Volvo B9TL with Alexander Dennis Enviro500 body, as it crosses the Grade II listed Felmersham Bridge, built around 1818, over the River Great Ouse in Bedfordshire as it takes up a school service. New in 2005 to Dublin Bus as VT5 (05 D 70005), it is one of two in the Northamptonshire operator's fleet. See p28.* JOHN ROBINSON

BACK COVER (UPPER): *A 1981 Leyland Leopard with 1992 East Lancs EL2000 body in the East Yorkshire fleet. See p88.* JOHN WHITEING

BACK COVER (LOWER): *Guards of London had the Park Royal body on AEC Bridgemaster ex-demonstrator 80 WMH rebuilt in the 1970s as a replica vintage bus. See p36.* PETER ROWLANDS

Published by Key Books
An imprint of Key Publishing Ltd
PO Box 100
Stamford
Lincs PE9 1XQ

www.keypublishing.com

ISBN: 978 1 80282 804 7

Design: SJmagic DESIGN SERVICES, India

Printed in Malta by Melita Press
Paola. Pla 3000
Malta. Europe

All rights reserved. No part of this book may be reproduced or transmitted in any form or by any means, electronic or mechanical, including photocopying, recording or by any information storage and retrieval system without permission from the publisher in writing.

© Key Publishing Ltd 2023

www.keybuses.com

The modern mix in Bournemouth includes Go South Coast's Purbeck Breezer service on which part open-top 1704 (HJ16 HSZ), a Volvo B5TL with MCV EvoSeti body, was negotiating St Peters Roundabout. See p16. MARK LYONS

Wheel of change

Welcome to the combination of nostalgia and current affairs that makes up this 2024 edition of *Buses Yearbook*.

Nostalgia helps us better understand current affairs, reminding us that today's new ideas might well have been tried before in different ways for different times. Our cover picture is of a new identity that will soon become familiar: the pale yellow Bee Network livery that Transport for Greater Manchester (TfGM) is rolling out as buses in the city region are transformed from a deregulated regime to London-style franchising, with services specified by the transport authority.

Franchising is new and Greater Manchester is the first place to implement it, but city-wide network identities are not, as a look back to the cover of *Buses Annual 1975* proves. That showed the striking identity of TfGM's predecessor of half a century ago, Selnec PTE, which merged 11 municipal fleets into one with a bright orange livery. As Roger Davies suggests on p64 in his look back to the 1960s and 1970s, orange may have been chosen because it was neither red, green nor blue and broke with the past of its constituent parts.

TfGM's objectives are similar to Selnec's: to create a unified, integrated public transport network. Future commentators and historians will be able to judge whether it succeeds in those aims, but Bob Hind's recent travels in Belfast and Dublin, described in his article starting on p120, reveal possible benefits from a unified network.

Change is a theme throughout this edition. We look at Bournemouth following the demise of Yellow Buses, the twists and turns in the 30 years since the London Buses companies were privatised, East Yorkshire in its early years as a management buyout with a bewitching variety of vehicles, Devon General when it was under the thumb of Western National, Northampton when the town had corporation buses and a deep devotion to Daimlers, McGill's

when it was owned by a family of that name, and the succession of operators on two routes on the edge of the Derbyshire Peaks.

John Robinson opens our eyes to the possibilities and pitfalls of one of the latest developments in photography: the ability to fly a camera in a drone to take pictures from above. He explains how to do it, how to keep on the right side of the law and how to avoid crashing it into deep water.

Another of our expert lensmen, Tony Wilson, takes us back over the 50-year lifespan, so far, of Showbus, which grew from a small event staged by students into the biggest British bus and coach rally to entertain the thousands of enthusiasts who took themselves to its various venues.

Besides the authors and photographers credited along with their work, two others deserve special mention once more for the skills they have deployed to restore and enhance some of the pictures published this year: Mike Eyre for those accompanying Roger Davies's article and Peter Rowlands who, in addition to penning his own description of some highly unusual vehicles, has worked his magic on several in other articles.

I hope you enjoy the varied articles that follow and find parallels between yesterday and today. ∎

Alan Millar

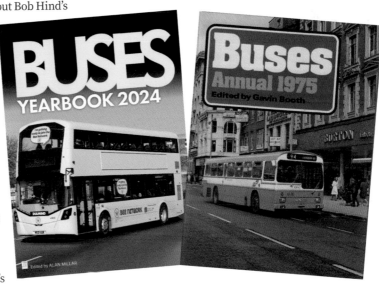

Birth of the Bee Network

In one of the biggest changes in bus service provision since 1986, Greater Manchester is moving from deregulation to franchising. **ALAN MILLAR** looks at what is happening and the politics that have led up to it

First Manchester 39257 (BT66 MRU), a Volvo B5LH with Wright Gemini 3 body for the Leigh guided busway, promoting public consultation on the Bee Network in St Peters Square, Manchester in October 2021. RUSSELL YOUNG

At the same time as this book goes on sale in September 2023, the initial phase of the franchising of Greater Manchester's bus services will be implemented, marking the first reversal of the deregulated system that has held across Britain outside London since October 1986.

In place of the separate identities of different bus operators — to describe them as competitors is no longer accurate — there will be just one, the yellow of the Bee Network, the name Transport for Greater Manchester (TfGM) has given the new system, taking its name from the insect that is a symbol of Manchester. A livery closely aligned to that of TfGM's Metrolink trams and one that gives its transport system a renewed sense of place.

For politicians in the conurbation, this has been a long desired objective. Indeed they never wanted deregulation to happen at all. Commercial operators, to put it mildly, are unconvinced that franchising is the right way forward, but they are learning to live with the new regime. Some of its most vocal past critics are making the best of it.

The rise and fall of PTEs

To understand what is being created and why, we need to go back briefly to the 1960s when an incoming Labour government, wanting to improve the image and delivery of public transport and passionate in its belief that the best transport systems were integrated ones, created passenger transport authorities and executives for the biggest city regions outside London.

Two of the first four were in north-west England — Merseyside around Liverpool and the Wirral, and Selnec which was short for South-east Lancashire, north-east Cheshire and covered the towns around Manchester. The other two were on Tyneside and

Bullock's of Cheadle was one of the longer lasting independent competitors, which sold most of its bus operations to Stagecoach in 2008. This was Piccadilly in Manchester in June 1995, with an MCW Metrorider of GMS following L20 BUL, an East Lancs-bodied Volvo Olympian that Bullock's bought new in 1993. IAIN MacGREGOR

in the West Midlands. All came into operation between October 1969 and January 1970, absorbing all the municipal operators in their areas.

Selnec hoovered up more than any of the others, 11 ranging in size from mighty Manchester to the small Ramsbottom UDC on its north-eastern edge. It added Wigan in 1974 when local government changes expanded its area of responsibility and changed its name to Greater Manchester Transport. And it negotiated the purchase of most of North Western Road Car from the National Bus Company (NBC) in 1972 and the subsequent acquisition of the privately owned Lancashire United Transport.

Local government change also added two more PTEs in West and South Yorkshire, and one was created in Scotland, in Greater Glasgow, in 1973.

The idea was that they would promote the development of superior bus and rail services in their areas. The politicians who oversaw them also used them as ways of changing the lives of their constituents, and by the 1980s all six of the English PTEs were using ratepayers' money to subsidise their fares to greater or lesser degrees.

That put them on a collision course with the Conservative government elected in 1979 and which, in 1984, published a White Paper paving the way for a huge revolution in the organisation of services. Road service licensing would be abolished, state-owned operators — starting with NBC — would be privatised and municipalities and

PTEs would be required to restructure their bus operations as arm's length viable companies.

Integration was no longer to be encouraged. Instead, operators were to compete to provide profitable services, while PTEs and local authorities would seek tenders from operators to provide the essential unprofitable services at the keenest price. Subsidised cheap fares would become a thing of the past.

The politicians and many professionals in the PTEs were horrified and argued in vain against it, campaigning against it too with posters on buses and banners in public places, but the government's view prevailed and services were deregulated on October 26, 1986, around 55 years after a prewar government introduced a national system of regulation.

The level of opposition varied between the conurbations, but the opposition in Greater Manchester lasted longer and was expressed more vociferously and continuously than elsewhere, with Labour councillors and MPs hoping that each general election would bring a change of government and a reversal of policy. That happened neither in 1988 nor 1992, the Conservative victory in 1992 coming as a surprise not detected until the results started to be declared.

Deregulation dawns

When Greater Manchester PTE restructured its huge bus undertaking in October 1986 as Greater Manchester Buses — or GM Buses as it styled itself

— it cut the fleet by 450 to just over 2,000 vehicles, of which approaching 1,800 were double-deckers. Many of the surplus vehicles were released on the secondhand market.

Many found new owners, and quite a few of those were operators in Greater Manchester taking the opportunity to launch registered services in competition with GM Buses. Other participants in the deregulated market included Ribble, a soon-to-be-sold NBC company that spotted an opportunity to grow.

One of the most significant early entrants into the market, from January 1987, was Bee Line Buzz, a new venture by the BET group's United Transport, with high-frequency brand new minibuses on busy corridors. As soon as its plans became clear, GM Buses stocked up with its own rival minibus fleet which it branded as Little Gem. This was one of the early battles of deregulation but it was one that BET — until 1967 a major operator of buses in England and Wales — lost. Bee Line Buzz was sold to Ribble in 1988 and plans for similar services in other PTE areas were given up before they started.

New minibuses apart, what characterised those early years of deregulation, particularly in places like Greater Manchester, was newcomers' widespread use of secondhand vehicles — of which ex-PTE vehicles were probably the better examples — on busy corridors in which arguably too many vehicles chased a finite number of passengers, and services were chopped and changed with alarming and confusing regularity.

Competition helped achieve the government's primary objective of reducing the cost of subsidising bus services, but at that stage did little to improve quality or foster genuine innovation. Things improved later, but first impressions counted.

The negatives played into the local politicians' hands and strengthened their resistance to the next part of the government's agenda, the privatisation of the arm's length companies. There was no legislation to compel this, but there were carrots and sticks to encourage it. West Yorkshire and Tyne & Wear sold their companies, Yorkshire Rider and Busways, to employee buyouts in 1988 and 1989, and all of the others acquiesced along similar lines in the years soon after, except Greater Manchester which resisted even after the government threatened to remove two of the concessions that had worked elsewhere: keeping each company intact as a single entity and allowing a closed sale to employees.

Split in two

Consequently, GM Buses was split in 1993 into northern and southern companies, which traded with respective fleetnames GM North and GMS, and they were offered for sale on the open market. These drew bids from the big new groups, several

After acquiring the Queens Road operation from First, Go North West upgraded the fleet with newer vehicles transferred from other group companies. MCV EvoSeti-bodied Volvo B5LH 3051 (BG66 MHZ) was one of 20 of these hybrids cascaded from Go-Ahead London in 2022. RUSSELL YOUNG

of which were by then listed on the stock exchange to raise funds to expand.

When the bids came in, a management/employee bid prevailed at GMS, while British Bus — a group not listed on the stock market but with a war chest for expansion — looked set to acquire GM North. That caused horror all round in Manchester, not least because British Bus already had a substantial presence in the area through its ownership of North Western and Bee Line Buzz. A change of judgment ensued and both companies went to employee buyouts.

But both gained new owners during 1996, Stagecoach buying GMS and First acquiring GM North. Both went on to acquire many of the smaller operators that had come on the scene, but their stewardship of the two main companies in the years that followed would bring starkly different reactions from the politicians who still yearned to bring bus services back under their control.

The short version of this is that Stagecoach made a far better job of its business in the southern half of the region than First did in the north, and First's shortcomings provided continuing fuel for the fire that the politicians wanted to place under the legislation that brought deregulation in 1986.

When First began to sell underperforming businesses around the country, Stagecoach bought some of them including the depot at Wigan, which was added to Stagecoach Manchester in 2012.

Although First won the bid to operate Vantage-branded double-deckers on the Leigh guided

Andy Burnham, mayor of Greater Manchester.

busway from 2016, the group seemed set to quit Greater Manchester altogether in 2019. It sold Queens Road depot in Manchester to Go-Ahead Group, which set up a new Go North West company to manage and re-invigorate it and give it a new grey/blue livery with flashes of orange as a nod to the days of GMT and Selnec, and sold the modern depot in Bolton to Rotala-owned Diamond North West.

There was much expectation that Oldham depot would also be sold, completing the exit, but if there was a prospective deal it never happened and First clung on.

Momentum for change

First's retrenchment came as the momentum was building towards franchising, bringing in a London-style of operation in which operators bid for the right to operate specific routes to

Five of 100 BYD/Alexander Dennis Enviro400EV City electric double-deckers that TfGM has bought for the Bee Network.
ALEXANDER DENNIS

Driver recruitment advertising for its takeover of Bolton depot from Diamond on Go North West 3358 (YX06 CXO), a Wright Eclipse Gemini-bodied Volvo B9TL transferred from East Yorkshire. RUSSELL YOUNG

the standards laid down by the local transport authority, which in this case is TfGM.

The big operators, Stagecoach especially, were as vociferous in their opposition to this as the politicians had been to deregulation and privatisation. And there was a big difference from London where the transport authority had never lost control of service specifications to the operators. The operators, who had paid handsomely to buy their Manchester subsidiaries, saw this as confiscation of their right to operate and earn revenue.

That momentum gathered pace with the election of a mayor for Greater Manchester, Labour's ex-government minister Andy Burnham, in 2017. He made little secret that he favoured franchising, although TfGM and the combined authority went through a process of consultation and evaluation before pressing ahead.

Further momentum came from a less predictable source. Shortly after becoming prime minister in 2019, the Conservatives' Boris Johnson gave a policy speech in Manchester that covered a wide range of objectives and areas, one of which was to endorse Burnham's plan for bus franchising.

In his eight years as mayor of London in 2008-16, Johnson had become familiar with how bus services were run there. Perhaps also his party now saw more merit in a system in which operators competed for the right to provide services, rather than one in which they gained a near monopoly.

Before it acquired First's business in Bolton, Diamond as a relatively small operator sounded enthusiastic about its potential to grow by winning contracts for franchised services. Its position changed once it had something big that it was at risk of losing and it became one of the strongest opponents of TfGM's plans, seeking a judicial review that it hoped — in vain as it turned out — would block the change.

Three phases

That was the point when any industry resistance became futile. The Bee Network — a name eventually to apply to all of the conurbation's public transport and active travel — would go ahead, with franchised buses introduced in three phases: on September 24, 2023; March 24, 2024; and January 5, 2025.

The results of the first two rounds show that the effect on the operators will be little short of seismic. In Phase 1 covering Wigan, Bolton, parts of Salford and Bury, Go North West is the winner, taking over Bolton depot from Diamond and operations — possibly also the depot — in Wigan from Stagecoach.

While Diamond loses its showpiece depot and becomes a smaller player, it nonetheless has won work requiring an investment in over 60 new single-deckers for the routes it has gained or retained. The shock of the change also caused it to lose drivers ahead of the change, withdraw routes at short notice and for Go North West to provide replacement cover and draft in buses to operate them.

Having made a big investment in new Wright StreetDeck double-deckers to replace the fleet of older vehicles that it chose not to buy from First in 2019, Diamond found many were now surplus to its requirements and transferred them to the Midlands. Those that are staying in Bolton were among the first recipients of Bee Network livery.

One hundred new BYD/Alexander Dennis Enviro400EV City electric double-deckers form part of the new regime, purchased by TfGM, but among others that Go-Ahead repainted yellow ready to be moved to Manchester were 14-year-old specially purchased Scania OmniCity double-deckers new to RATP London. They are sound vehicles, but we can only guess quite how the ordinary folk of Greater Manchester might react to realising that their super new bus network has what they might see as London cast-offs.

If Phase 1 left Go-Ahead elated and Stagecoach despondent at losing Wigan, then Phase 2 turned the tables. This covers Oldham, Rochdale, parts of Bury, Salford and north Manchester. Stagecoach is the big winner with this, retaining the depot it already had in Middleton (taken over with the Bluebird business) and gaining Manchester Queens Road from Go North West and Oldham from First. Diamond has also won some of this work, and First retains a reduced presence with other gains.

On that basis, the outcome of bids for Phase 3 is impossible to predict. This takes in the area where Stagecoach has held sway since 1996. It covers Stockport, Tameside, Trafford and the rest of Manchester and Salford. Stagecoach opened a new south Manchester depot at Sharston in 2011, has deployed electric double-deckers on key corridors and in 2022 announced a major investment in new Volvo BZL electrics for Stockport. Whether it gets to operate them is another question.

What also remains to be seen is whether the Bee Network will succeed in attracting more people on to public transport without compelling current bus users to change mid-journey on to Metrolink.

But with other city regions, especially Liverpool, keen to follow Greater Manchester's example and take control of their buses, many will be looking closely to see how it all works out. ■

A Scania OmniCity new to London United and acquired from Stephensons of Essex for the Bee Network, operating temporarily with Go South Coast in Bournemouth in the summer of 2023 as 1179 (YT59 PCF). MARK LYONS

On track to **build buses**

MIKE FENTON tells the story of two railway rolling stock manufacturers that diversified for a time into bus and coach products, one of them even building its own chassis

Readers of a certain age may well recall the Burt Bacharach/Hal David song *Trains and Boats and Planes*, which was a hit for Billy J Kramer and The Dakotas in 1965 and Dionne Warwick in 1966. So, having covered in *Yearbook* 2022 bodybuilders that began as makers of planes and in 2023 ones that had been builders of boats, how could I not now address the trains aspect?

My story begins with the Gloucester Wagon Company, established in 1860 as a manufacturer of railway equipment with an initial capital of £100,000. Twenty-eight years later, at a meeting held on August 28, 1888 at the Bell Hotel, Gloucester, the company was wound up voluntarily and reconstructed as the Gloucester Railway Carriage and Wagon Company, registered on September 14 that same year.

Although essentially a builder of railway rolling stock, in its early years the firm also produced horse buses, horse trams and various other horse-drawn conveyances. Then in 1908, in complete contrast, an ornate open-top double-deck body was built on a Clarkson steamer, this being displayed at Olympia in London from March 26 to April 4 that year.

That apart, bus bodybuilding began in earnest in 1932, with the bodying of Thornycroft DD/RC6 double-deck demonstrator CG 1126 along with 11 normal control Thornycroft BC 26-seaters for the local Gloucester Corporation. These were 20-30 (FH 7948-58), entering service between November 1932 and January 1933, followed in July 1933 by six 32-seat BC Forward models as 31-6 (FH 8289-94).

The year 1933 also saw the introduction of the forward-control Gloster Gardner type of 17ft 6in wheelbase, powered by the frugal Gardner 6LW oil engine — the term at the time for diesel — driving through a five-speed overdrive gearbox. It had been designed in conjunction with the Watts family, owner of Red & White Services, and the first six, with 30-seat coach bodies, were put to work on the

operator's South Wales-London services between July and November 1933.

Despite their economy of operation, only three others were built: WN 6536 and WN 7126 for Neath & Cardiff Luxury Coaches and WN 6823 for V Williams (Richmond Motor Services) of Neath, all in 1934 and all with 32-seat Gloucester-built coach bodies.

Disappointing as sales of Gloster Gardner coaches must have been, they were better than those of Gloster trolleybuses, which got no farther than a prototype TDD double-decker fitted with a 54-seat all-metal centre-entrance body. It was exhibited at the 1933 Commercial Motor Show at Olympia and although having several advanced features — notably a low floor made possible by having its motor at the rear — orders were not forthcoming. After the show, it went on hire to Southend Corporation as 122 (JN 3822), where it remained from purchase in December 1934 to the end of 1949.

Bodybuilding continues

Although the production of Gloster chassis ceased in 1934, bodies continued to be built on other makes, with Gloucester Corporation taking a final two Thornycroft BC Forward 32-seaters as 37/8 (FH 8765/6).

Also in 1934, a 48-seat double-deck Gloucester body was built on a Morris Commercial Imperial chassis as Birmingham City Transport 506 (OC 506), two 51-seat lightweight bodies framed in pitch pine were built for Walsall Corporation on Dennis Lance II chassis — 103/4 (ADH 974/5) — and Aberdare Urban District Council had a Daimler COG5 fitted with a 48-seat double-deck body, 3 (TG 8618).

Aberdare then took seven more Daimler COG5 double-deckers in 1935, this time with 52-seat bodies, 4-10 (TG 9441-7), plus a pair of 32-seat, dual-door single-deckers also on COG5 chassis, 25/6 (TG 9448/9). A further two double-deckers were built for Walsall on Dennis Lance II chassis,

105/6 (BDH 973/4), and finally a 32-seat rear entrance coach body was fitted to an Albion Valiant SpPV71 chassis for Red & White, entering service in August 1935 as 255 (AAX 130).

After building 48 bus and coach bodies, the company concentrated then on building railway rolling stock, with a workforce that in 1937 totalled 2,400 employees. During World War Two it built 764 Churchill tanks between 1941 and 1945 as well as prefabricated sections for the Mulberry Harbours, used to great effect in the D-Day landings in Normandy in June 1944.

The production of railway rolling stock resumed postwar, then in December 1961 the company was acquired by Winget of Rochester, Kent and renamed the Gloucester Engineering Company. A period of decline followed, with the last railway carriage built in 1963 and the last wagon in 1968, and although it continued to make railway-related products for several more years, closure came in 1986.

ABOVE: *The last Gloucester RC&W-bodied bus to be built, in August 1935, was this 32-seat rear-entrance coach on a Gardner 6LW diesel-engined Albion Valiant SpPV71 for Red & White, photographed at Cheltenham coach station.*
JF HIGHAM/THE BUS ARCHIVE

RIGHT: *Of the nine Gloster Gardners built, Red & White took the first six in 1933, all with rear-entrance Gloucester coach bodies, as shown by this view of 227 (WO 7615) in wartime condition, with white-edged wings and masked headlights.*
AUTHOR'S COLLECTION

ABOVE: *Birmingham City Transport's 51 Morris Commercial Imperial double-deckers was the largest fleet of them in the country, although whether that would have been the case had they not been built in the city is questionable. The only one with a Gloucester body was 506 (OC 506), photographed at Hamstead Hill in 1938 when four years old.* RT COXON

ABOVE: *Walsall Corporation 104 (ADH 975) was one of a pair of 51-seat Gloucester-bodied Dennis Lance II double-deckers that entered service in July 1934. It was withdrawn in 1945 and sold for scrap.* THE BUS ARCHIVE

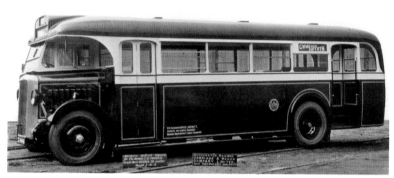

LEFT: *Manufacturers' works views can be sterile; but with this view of Aberdare UDC 25 (TG 9448), one of two Daimler COG5 chassis with Gloucester 32-seat dual-door bodies supplied in May 1935, it comes with a wealth of information shown on the two boards: order number, build date, seating capacity and unladen weight, which was 5ton 10cwt 3qtr, or 5,626kg in metric.* ROY MARSHALL COLLECTION/ THE BUS ARCHIVE

Hurst Nelson

The Hurst Nelson company came into being in 1880 when John J Hurst and Andrew S Nelson entered into partnership in Glasgow as railway wagon builder Hurst, Nelson & Company. In 1893 Glasgow-born railway builder and civil engineer Charles de Neuville Forman joined the firm, which was then incorporated as a limited company by the same name.

By then production had been transferred to a new factory around 15miles south-east in Motherwell, built alongside the Caledonian Railway's Glasgow-Carlisle line. Soon after, in 1896, Hurst left the business, selling his shares to Forman, although Forman's involvement did not last for much longer, as he died aged only 48 on February 8, 1901.

Later, for financial reasons, it became necessary to reconstruct the company, hence on February 16, 1909 the original Hurst, Nelson & Company business was liquidated, with its assets transferred to a new company registered under the same name, on the same day, with an increased capital of £320,000.

Although best known as a builder of railway rolling stock, with an estimated production of 50,000 wagons, it also built tramcars from around 1900 to 1928, with more than 600 built entirely at its works, plus another 1,200 or so bodied on other makers' frames. The four cars on the cable-hauled Great Orme Tramway in Llandudno were built by Hurst Nelson and have been in near continuous service since they were delivered in 1902.

The building of bodies for buses and trolleybuses comprised only a small part of its activities, with most of the former being 34-seat open-top double-deck Clarkson steamers built between 1909 and 1917 for the National Steam Car Company of Chelmsford. Although none ran beyond 1919, their bodies survived, and many were transferred to other vehicles. As for the trolleybuses, there were just six 28-seat Railless vehicles bodied in 1911 for the pioneering systems in Leeds (four) and Bradford (two).

No other road-going passenger vehicles were bodied by Hurst Nelson until 1932 when Glasgow

Corporation, which had bought 30 Hurst Nelson-bodied trams in 1928, had a new 51-seat double-deck body built on 188 (GE 7220), an accident-damaged Leyland Titan TD1 of 1930, this being unusual in having an emergency exit, complete with ladder, incorporated into the upstairs front window.

Finally, between November 1932 and January 1933, nine Crossley Condors with more conventional 52-seat bodies entered service as Manchester Corporation 381-9 (XJ 2260-8), at which time 218 bodies of all kinds had been built.

Following railway nationalisation in January 1948, wagon sales declined markedly and after making a substantial loss in the 1957/58 financial year, the Motherwell works was closed down and the business sold to Charles Roberts & Company of Wakefield, coincidentally another railway rolling stock business that had been a builder of bus bodies. ∎

ABOVE: *This photograph of Manchester Corporation Crossley Condor 382 (XJ 2261) was taken at the Hurst Nelson works towards the end of 1932. With the background removed, the image was used in the bodybuilder's advertisements until at least December 1933, by which time the piano-front style of double-decker had become outdated.* GREATER MANCHESTER TRANSPORT SOCIETY

BELOW: *Glasgow Corporation 1115, preserved at Crich Tramway Village, is one of 30 double-bogie 68-seat trams that Hurst Nelson bodied in 1928.* ALAN MILLAR

The coast with More

A year after Yellow Buses ceased operations, MARK LYONS explains how services have developed in the Bournemouth area where Go South Coast's Morebus has strengthened its dominant position

Bournemouth Corporation trolleybus 280 (YLJ 280), a Sunbeam MF2B with 63-seat Weymann body, at Iford in 1966. Bournemouth specified an unusual layout for its trolleybuses and motorbuses at the time, with passengers entering by an open platform and staircase at the rear, and exiting by a front staircase and enclosed platform. GEOFFREY MORANT

Bournemouth — whose present day council promotes itself as 'The Coast with the Most' — was one of those places, like London and Edinburgh, where the buses helped define the urban landscape. Its yellow fleet, complementing the 7mile sweep of the town's sandy beach, was familiar to generations of residents and visitors alike.

The Yellow Buses story began in 1902 when Bournemouth Corporation started operating electric trams. Its first motorbus services followed in 1906, initially to feed passengers on to trams. Services expanded to cover most of Bournemouth and parts of neighbouring Christchurch.

Following early experiments, trolleybuses replaced the trams between 1934 and 1936, and by 1951, when the final extension opened, the trolleybus network covered nearly 30 route miles. Bournemouth took delivery of the last

new trolleybuses built for a UK operator, in 1962. However, only one year later the corporation took the first steps towards abandoning trolleybuses and the last examples ran on April 20, 1969.

The trams, trolleybuses and motorbuses had always featured yellow in their livery and in 1982 the council adopted Yellow Buses as a fleetname. When it sold the majority of shares in what since deregulation in October 1986 had been an arm's length company, Bournemouth Transport, to Transdev in 2005, a condition of sale was that the brand was retained.

On March 3, 2011 the company became part of RATP Group as a consequence of that group's exit from its part ownership of Transdev, both RATP and Transdev being French multinational transport groups. RATP sold Yellow Buses to its directors in July 2019.

New to Yellow Buses in 2015, when French state company RATP owned the business, was VGW198 (BF15 KFK), a Volvo B5TL with Wright Gemini 3 body. MARK LYONS

Hants & Dorset to More

The other major operator in the area was Hants & Dorset which began life in 1916 as Bournemouth & District Motor Services. When Poole Borough Council decided to replace its trams, it entered into an agreement with Hants & Dorset to operate motorbuses over the routes. The company also ran services linking Bournemouth with towns in the surrounding area although, for many years, its buses were not allowed to carry passengers on local journeys within Bournemouth.

It also operated to Weymouth and Salisbury on routes run jointly run with Southern (later Western) National and Wilts & Dorset respectively. Hants & Dorset's buses were green until 1972 when it adopted National Bus Company (NBC) poppy red. This was, in part, a gesture towards former Wilts & Dorset staff, as Hants & Dorset had recently completed a protracted absorption of its smaller northern neighbour which had run red buses.

When NBC split Hants & Dorset into smaller units in 1983, it resurrected the Wilts & Dorset name for services in the Bournemouth, Poole, Swanage, Lymington and Salisbury areas. Wilts & Dorset was sold to its management in June 1987. Go-Ahead Group bought the company in August 2003 to form the nucleus of its Go South Coast business today.

That placed new pressure on Yellow Buses, which had faced several competitive onslaughts in its traditional operating area since deregulation.

Go-Ahead already owned the former NBC and municipal bus operations in Brighton and expressed an interest in buying Yellow Buses from the council, stating that it would develop an integrated bus network for the area.

While that offer was rejected, Wilts & Dorset won a contract in autumn 2004 to provide services on behalf of Bournemouth University, work previously undertaken by Yellow Buses, and in December that year it launched its More brand in Bournemouth and Poole, with a fleet of 30 new Wright Eclipse Urban-bodied Volvo B7RLE single-deckers operating two simplified routes — m1 and m2 — between the towns in place of the five subtly different services it ran before.

The More brand — known within the company as Morebus — gradually replaced the Wilts & Dorset name in the Bournemouth area, while services to Swanage were branded as Purbeck Breezer

Yellow Buses collapses

Yellow Buses survived for only three years as a management buyout. The Covid pandemic, which struck within the buyout's first year, did not help, but the company was already struggling financially and administrators were appointed on July 29, 2022, a few weeks after it had celebrated 120 years of operation. All services ceased running on August 4.

Recognising that all was not well with its neighbour, Go South Coast had plans in place to

The red notice on the front grille of ECW-bodied Bristol Lodekka LD6B 1365 (RLJ 515) makes clear that passengers may not use this Hants & Dorset double-decker for local journeys within Bournemouth. This June 1970 view shows it on the top floor of the two-level bus and coach station in Bournemouth town centre. GEOFFREY MORANT

Go South Coast 225 (HF67 EUH), an Alexander Dennis Enviro200 MMC, operating More trunk service m1 in Bournemouth. MARK LYONS

step in and provide a service on most of the network two days after the collapse. The administrators sold the coach operations to National Express, but were unable to find a buyer for the core bus business and arranged for most of the fleet to be sold individually.

As soon as that became clear, Go South Coast announced plans to operate over most of Yellow Buses' commercial network and retained the familiar route numbers. The main exceptions were sections of route where Morebus already provided services, such as between Bournemouth and Poole, and Yellow

The Go South Coast vehicles operating the Unibus services to the University of Bournemouth wear a variety of colourful liveries. The front half of this one on Alexander Dennis Enviro400 MMC 1623 (HF66 CDY) in Christchurch evokes memories of the yellow municipal operation. MARK LYONS

Buses' route 3 (Westbourne-Royal Bournemouth Hospital) which was covered by existing route m1 (Poole-Royal Bournemouth Hospital). The m1 had recently been extended to the hospital in one of the final competitive moves against Yellow Buses.

It also announced that it would provide a service over three routes previous run under contract for Bournemouth, Christchurch & Poole Council — the 18 (West Way-Bournemouth), 33 (Christchurch-Bournemouth) and 36 (Kinson-Talbot View Estate) pending retendering, after which Eastleigh-based Xelabus took them over from August 15 on a six-month emergency contract. Xelabus bought the collapsed company's Yellow Coaches name.

The expanded network required around 40 extra buses and Go South Coast transferred vehicles in from its Salisbury Reds, Swindon Buses and Bluestar operations. Fortuitously, it had also taken delivery of 19 new Alexander Dennis Enviro400 double-deckers for the Bournemouth University contract and instead of being cascaded elsewhere within Go South Coast, the previous fleet stayed in Bournemouth.

Xelabus closed its Bournemouth operation in early 2023 and Morebus took over the contracts for routes 18, 33 and 36.

Go South Coast was expanding on another front by then, with Bluestar filling the void left by First

Bus's closure of its Southampton operations in February 2023. Go South Coast's Bluestar took back the buses it had loaned to Morebus, their place in Bournemouth taken by five Wright Eclipse Gemini-bodied Volvo B7TLs that had been new to Go-Ahead London but operated latterly with Go North East.

A yellow renaissance

Go South Coast launched an expanded range of services in 2023 for summer visitors to the area. These built upon the Breezer brand for the Purbeck routes and included two seafront routes branded Beach Breezer.

Vehicles used on these included the only ex-Yellow Buses vehicles that it had acquired, two open-top East Lancs Vyking-bodied Volvo B7TLs. They were given a yellow and blue vinyl wrap. The company's established service 60 (Rockley-Sandbanks), which skirts Poole Harbour, was branded Harbour Breezer.

Pending delivery of new Alexander Dennis Enviro400s, and to boost capacity over the summer, at least 13 Scania OmniCity double-deckers, new to RATP London United, were acquired from Stephensons of Essex. Bournemouth was not their primary destination, as they form part of the fleet that Go North West was building up for the Bee Network contracts in Greater Manchester and some entered service in the pale yellow livery for that work, adding another hue to the area's streets and a variation on the traditional theme of yellow.

Although it now provides the overwhelming majority of services across the Bournemouth, Christchurch and Poole conurbation, Go South Coast does not have a total monopoly. First Hampshire & Dorset's service X54 (Poole-Weymouth) operates under its Jurassic Coaster brand, while Discover Dorset operates a hop-on/hop-off sightseeing service for City Sightseeing.

Transpora, which probably by chance has a presence in several other English places with an

Wright Eclipse Gemini-bodied Volvo B7TL 6916 (LX06 EBZ) providing former Yellow Buses route 1a, with More fleetnames applied to its Go North East livery. When new in 2006, it was Go-Ahead London WVL267. MARK LYONS

Operating tendered service 33 between Christchurch and Bournemouth and with vinyls to show that it is one of the additional vehicles drafted into the Morebus fleet was 2704 (YX64 VOF), an Alexander Dennis Enviro200 still in the park-&-ride livery of Salisbury Reds, another part of the former Wilts & Dorset business. MARK LYONS

Morebus acquired two Volvo B7TLs with convertible open-top East Lancs Vyking bodies from Yellow Buses to operate its rebranded Beach Breezer service, which keeps a few of its Bournemouth buses yellow. This is 1813 with cherished registration YBZ 224 applied by its former owner. MARK LYONS

Transpora GX09 ZZW, one of the Wright Eclipse Gemini 2-bodied Volvo B9TLs operated successively by Bus Vannin, Yellow Buses and Xelabus. It retained Yellow Buses' final livery when photographed in 2023. MARK LYONS

initial letter B (Blackpool, Bath, Bristol), provides schools services in Bournemouth and launched an open-top service between Bournemouth Pier and Hengistbury Head at Easter 2023. It added a Bournemouth-Boscombe local bus service in June the same year.

The Transpora fleet includes two Wright Eclipse Gemini 2-bodied Volvo B9TLs, new to Bus Vannin in the Isle of Man, which Yellow Buses acquired during its brief period in management ownership. Xelabus operated them after Yellow Buses collapsed and they retain their yellow livery. ◼

Putting on a **brave front**

GAVIN BOOTH provides a selection of examples of how Edinburgh's principal operator has featured vehicles in the printed publicity it has produced to promote its services

Younger readers used to checking bus times on their computers, laptops, mobile phones – perhaps even watches – may be surprised to learn that there was a time when most people relied on the printed word for this information.

Enthusiasts of a certain age dutifully toured bus company and bus station offices gathering handfuls of printed leaflets to plan their travels or simply keep up with what was going on. They could buy chunky timetable books where these were produced, or collect free leaflets.

This is what I did in Edinburgh over the past seven decades, to my wife's occasional dismay, although she may have noticed that the Covid pandemic has caused many bus, tram and indeed train operators to cut back on the production of these, in the knowledge that most people have access to more up-to-date information electronically.

Living in a city with an impressive network of bus services, with detailed information on times and fares at every stop, I rarely need to check bus times online, but I must confess that an app that tells me where every bus is, by fleetnumber, is a thing of wonder. Normally I have preferred the thrill of the chase, but there are times when it has made the chase much easier.

There are several themes in this selection of Edinburgh Corporation and Lothian leaflet covers – how a greater awareness of good graphic design developed, how images of buses have been used to support the message, and, intriguingly, how often the buses featured have been from small non-representative batches. ■

The 1956 cover on this page is an example of the simple black-and-white leaflets of the time; this one is of particular interest as it announces new bus routes 23 and 28 that started operating on the day following the operation of the 23 and 28 trams, Edinburgh's last first-generation trams, the previous evening.

Ken Cameron's picture of a 28 at the Braids terminus shows 795, a Metro-Cammell Orion-bodied Leyland PD2/20 new in October 1957, one of 11 similar buses operated unpainted — other than a madder band between the decks — until 1959.

The joy of pocket-size leaflets is that you can stuff your pockets with them, unlike the massive tomes my old employer, the Scottish Bus Group, produced for many years. There was a view that timetables should be paid for and were to be consulted at home. Certainly you would have needed large pockets to accommodate this 1970 timetable for Eastern Scottish, the other Edinburgh-based bus operator. Admittedly, for sixpence (33p at today's values) you got 416 pages of times and a fold-out map, but most purchasers only wanted to know about local services.

CITY AND ROYAL BURGH OF EDINBURGH
TRANSPORT DEPARTMENT

Bus Services Nos. 23 and 28

BUS SERVICE No. 23—Route
MORNINGSIDE STATION, MORNINGSIDE ROAD, BRUNTS-FIELD PLACE, TOLLCROSS, LAURISTON PLACE, GEORGE IV BRIDGE, BANK STREET, MOUND, HANOVER STREET, DUNDAS STREET, PITT STREET, CANONMILLS, INVERLEITH ROW, INVERLEITH GARDENS to GRANTON ROAD STATION.

BUS SERVICE No. 28—Part Day only and does not operate on Sundays—Route
BRAIDS (Braid Hills Road), COMISTON ROAD, MORNINGSIDE ROAD, BRUNTSFIELD PLACE, TOLLCROSS, LOTHIAN ROAD, PRINCES STREET, LEITH STREET, LEITH WALK, PILRIG STREET, NEWHAVEN ROAD, STANLEY ROAD, CRAIGHALL ROAD to NEWHAVEN.

Commencing Saturday, 17th November 1956

Transport Office,
2 St. James' Square,
Edinburgh, 1.

W. M. LITTLE,
Transport Manager.

November, 1956.

ROBERT MITCHELL & SONS, Printers, EDINBURGH

Coach tours have been an important source of revenue for Edinburgh Corporation and Lothian for more than a century and charabancs in the 1920s were followed by 'all-weather' coaches from the 1930s.

By the 1950s there was a demand for larger coaches and Edinburgh converted 16 Leyland-bodied Royal Tigers from rear-entrance buses to fairly chunky front-entrance coaches, but as visitor numbers soared, investment in new 'proper' coaches in the 1960s brought a range of Duple-bodied Bedfords into the fleet, including 15 twin-steer VALs, as featured on a two-colour leaflet showing a 1964-delivered 52-seat VAL14 with the Vega Major body. My photograph shows one of these impressive beasts, 218, at Holyrood.

At the time, Edinburgh only operated tours within the city, ranging from a 1hr tour of the Royal Mile and Arthur's Seat to a three-hour Castle, Cathedral and Palace tour with conducted visits.

Local government reform meant that Edinburgh Corporation's transport department morphed into Lothian Region Transport in 1975, and bus deregulation turned it into an arm's length company 11 years later. This prompted a long series of leaflets for individual routes or, as in this case, groups of routes.

The corporation had introduced two weekend night services in 1925 to cater for shift workers and by 1999, when this leaflet was produced, the night network had grown to five or six services, with route numbers depending on the days travelled. Since then Lothian's night bus network has grown considerably, broadly following main daytime routes, using the day route numbers with an N prefix.

The bus chosen to represent the night service operation was one of Lothian's 12 two-door Leyland Lynx 2s, new in 1991 and sold somewhat prematurely in 2000. One of them, 188, is preserved today, restored to its original condition.

An interesting addition to the Lothian tour fleet in 2000 was this Leyland Leopard with semi open-top Alexander Y-type body that had started life in 1977 with Western SMT and had been used by Stagecoach on the Isle of Arran.

A 49-seater, it had 16 seats in the forward covered section and 33 in the open rear. Painted white with tartan waistband and skirt – should you call a tartan skirt a kilt? – it was branded The Royal Park Charabanc and offered passengers 'the best panoramic views of the city' on a trip through Holyrood Park, where double-deckers were not normally allowed.

The cover of the leaflet promoting the 50min tour featured the Leopard by Dunsapie Loch in the park, with views over the north of Edinburgh towards the Firth of Forth. The tour was fairly short-lived and the Leopard was eventually sold in 2008. My photograph shows it, complete with tartan seats, at Our Dynamic Earth, one of the city's newer tourist attractions.

Lothian was a late convert to the integral Leyland National, avoiding the sometimes troublesome original variety but embracing the Mk2 version with its Leyland 680 engine, familiar in vertical form in Lothian's large fleet of Atlanteans.

However, fierce competition from First Edinburgh led to the appearance of 17 original-type Nationals in 2001, gathered from various sources. These were between 21 and 28 years old and had been retrofitted with Volvo engines. Originally intended as driver training buses, they quickly became battle buses when First started competing, and when the threat had receded they were withdrawn in 2003, clocking up two years' service.

This one survived long enough to appear on the cover of this 2002 leaflet – a 1979 vehicle that had been new to Central SMT. My photograph shows one of the 'newest', 1980 ex-Trent 128 at Ocean Terminal.

From 28 October 2002

40

Revised Timetable

Saturday journeys no longer operate. Minor changes to weekday service.

Frederick Street
≋ Waverley
Regent Road
Meadowbank
Mountcastle
Brunstane
Newcraighall
Stoneybank
Musselburgh

Lothian Buses
–your locally owned buses

☎ **0131 555 6363**
www.lothianbuses.co.uk
Issue 2

Unlike many fleets, Lothian decided that minibuses were not the answer in the uncertain years following deregulation in 1986. It did the opposite, continuing to invest instead in longer Leyland double-deckers with up to 81 seats from 1988 when many operators were still cautiously watching the market before investing in new vehicles.

But when Lothian won contracts for services using residential streets in the east of the city, it looked around for suitable smaller buses and in 2003 came up with three former Stagecoach 1990 Mercedes-Benz 709Ds with 25-seat Alexander AM-type bodies, as here on the cover of a 2004 leaflet for the 60/69 Monday-Saturday daytime routes and in the picture taken at King's Road, Portobello. Lothian operated supported services under the Mac Tours name, with buses in a red/cream livery.

The last of these little Mercs was withdrawn in 2008.

Lothian's timetable booklet covering its Christmas and New Year services provided an annual opportunity for designers to come up with something festively different.

For its 2004/05 cover, it featured a bus hanging from a Christmas tree, but it was not just any bus. It was not even a Lothian bus, but it was a bus that was operating for Lothian on extended loan. It was a 2004 Scania N94UD OmniDekka with 90-seat East Lancs body, and had received Lothian's Harlequin livery displaying the temporary fleetnumber 999. My photograph shows it in Princes Street in the heart of the city centre.

After leaving Edinburgh, it went on to operate with several independent operators in England, rebuilt as a convertible open-topper. Lothian did buy 15 Scania double-deckers in 2006/07, but these were the Polish-built OmniCity model; these included the first production examples of a model that became popular, particularly with London United and East London Bus Group.

Lothian's first diesel-electric hybrids were 15 Alexander Dennis Enviro400H 80-seat double-deckers delivered in 2011 and part-funded by the Scottish government. It promoted them with this teaser leaflet that used the slogans that appeared on the buses – be ahead, be smart, be daring, be bold, be different.

The buses were certainly different and wore a livery in Lothian's then-standard style, but using different colours – metallic radiance/ winter gold – and carrying the fleetname ecoLothianbuses.com, as shown in 2012 as 214 invited passengers to 'be daring' in Princes

Street. They were subsequently repainted into the standard madder/white livery, converted to run on pure diesel, and were sold in 2023, passing to Wellglade companies TM Travel and Notts & Derby.

Lothian went on to buy more hybrids, though from its then current main supplier, Volvo. It bought 7900H single-deckers built in Poland and B5LH double-deckers with Wright Gemini 3 bodies. But its next major orders for double-deckers were for pure diesel-engined B5TLs, initially with Gemini 3 bodies and, most recently, Alexander Dennis 84-seat Enviro400 bodies.

This bus is different...

Something new is coming to service 10 from 11 September 2011...

ecoLothianbuses.com

For the cover of its 2011/12 Christmas and New Year timetable, Lothian made a festive nod to its Morningside Maisie branding of the 5 route.

At the time, Lothian was branding some of its principal routes with local references and earlier in 2011 Maisie MacKenzie, the cat featured in a series of books by local author/illustrator Aileen Paterson, became the face of the 5 route serving the Morningside area.

This was Maisie's second appearance on Lothian literature, this time in a kilted Santa outfit in seasonal snow. The Maisie branding was applied to ten 2011 Volvo B9TLs with Wright Eclipse Gemini 2 bodies; this had been discontinued by 2018 as Lothian moved away from route branding. My picture shows 955 at Northfield.

Christmas & New Year Buses

23 December 2011 to 4 January 2012

Merry Christmas

0131 555 6363 Lothianbuses.com

The first battery-electric bus to operate in Edinburgh was a Crompton-Leyland demonstrator with a Willowbrook body built on an FG light truck chassis in 1973, but it was 44 years before Lothian bought any new-generation electric buses.

In 2017 Wrightbus introduced the StreetAir DF, an electric single-decker based on its StreetDeck double-deck chassis, and available in 10.6m length. Lothian, then a good customer for Wright bodies, ordered six 27-seat StreetAirs, which arrived in 2017. They went into service on the 1 route, the direct descendent of Edinburgh Corporation's first motorbus route in 1919, and the cover of this 2018 timetable features one of them.

They were not particularly successful, apparently requiring extra recharging when heaters and windscreen wipers were in use, and were withdrawn from service in 2019. Wrightbus's new owner dropped the StreetAir and replaced it with a new range of Electroliner electric single-deckers and double-deckers. Mark Bailey's picture is of 286 at Holyrood on route 6.

In the 2010s Lothian Buses created two new entities for its networks of services well beyond the city boundaries, into East and West Lothian.

What started as East Lothian Buses in 2012 became East Coast Buses in 2016, with a green livery to stand out from the madder city buses. The East Lothian services eventually replaced First Scotland East services in that area, but the West Lothian services introduced in 2018 adopted Lothian Country branding, in competition with First.

Most West Lothian services were trunk routes connecting main centres of population with Edinburgh, but in 2019 two half-hourly express coach routes to Edinburgh were added, EX1 from Bathgate and EX2 from Linlithgow, both offering end-to-end journeys of approximately 45min. Branded Green Arrow, they used eight new Volvo B8Rs with a 49-seat Interurban variant of the Plaxton Leopard body with a centre wheelchair lift. The picture shows Linlithgow-bound 9205 in George Street in the city centre.

The Covid pandemic hastened the withdrawal of these routes and the eight Leopards passed into the grey-painted Lothian Motorcoaches fleet.

Eye in the sky

JOHN ROBINSON has taken to the air with a drone that allows him to photograph buses and coaches in the environment in which they operate. He shares his results and explains how to achieve the best effects while keeping on the right side of the law

Photography using drones — also known as unmanned aerial vehicles (UAVs) — has been possible for several years and is emerging rapidly as the favoured means of capturing scenes by an increasing number of photographers.

Although the camera technology on many consumer drones is only equivalent to that of a mobile phone, in my feature in *Buses Yearbook 2020* I demonstrated that perfectly acceptable images can be taken with such devices. Indeed, the race to provide ever-improving camera technology and features in phones shows no signs of abating. Many of the larger drones available, though, have cameras equivalent to professional digital single-lens reflex cameras.

Their use is already prevalent in landscape, maritime and railway photography, all of which are photographic genres I shoot. The use of what is effectively a flying camera allows photographs to be taken from otherwise impossible positions, such as over water or above inaccessible land, enabling fresh viewpoints to be opened up.

At the moment, it appears that only a few bus photographers use them. Being relatively small, buses are more difficult to photograph than those other subjects because if photographed from too far away they can be lost in the composition. Most of my transport photographs have always been of subjects in their environment, rather than pure record shots. Being able to get some height and width on the subject, which would not necessarily be possible to the same extent using other means such as a pole, enables even more of the environment to be included in the composition. While I have used poles in the past, since starting

This is a drone photographer's view of how a picture appears on the DJI Fly app. It was taken in June 2023 at Huddersfield bus station, the busiest in West Yorkshire and which opened in 1974. Most of the buses are in the First fleet, mainly Volvo B9TLs with Wright Eclipse Gemini 2 bodies in HD Connect and generic liveries as well as a Wright StreetLite and a Volvo B7RLE with Wright Eclipse Urban body. On stand Y nearest the camera, Arriva Yorkshire Alexander Dennis Enviro400 1928 in Max livery is about to leave for Leeds.

drone photography in March 2020, the pole has remained unused; indeed, a drone is a lot quicker to deploy than a pole and a great deal more portable.

Use of a drone may seem off-putting to some people, not only because of the attention it may arouse, particularly in areas like town centres, but also the confidence to fly it safely in such confined places. I was reticent about my own ability to fly one, having no previous experience with model aircraft, so before I purchased a serious drone I practised flying with a cheap toy one.

Satisfied that I could operate it confidently, I purchased a DJI Mavic Mini. As for attention from onlookers, wherever this has occurred it has always been a positive interaction where they are generally amazed when I show them the pictures on my phone.

Crucially, the DJI Mavic Mini weighs just beneath the 250g threshold, where restrictions on operating the aircraft are much less onerous than with drones above this weight.

Legal requirements

The Civil Aviation Authority (CAA) is responsible for managing the operation of drones and model aircraft in the United Kingdom and pilots must register with it. Two forms of identification (ID) are required, a flyer ID valid for five years and an operator ID valid for one year.

You must pass the CAA's official online multiple-choice theory test when first registering for and renewing a flyer ID. The operator ID is required for the person managing the drone, usually the flyer unless the drone is owned by a business where more than one person might fly it.

Because drone laws are evolving constantly, I do not propose to go into the full details here; prospective drone pilots should therefore check the latest legislation on resources such as the CAA website to ensure they are compliant.

However the basic rules, which all drone users must abide by, are that the maximum height which can be flown above ground level is 120m (approximately 400ft) and the drone has to be kept within visual line of sight (VLOS) at all times; in other words, it cannot be flown just by relying on the image on the controller screen.

Drones should never be flown in flight restrictions zones (FRZs) such as around airports, military establishments and prisons, unless permission has been sought and granted. Helpfully, several apps are available which show the up-to-date status of all airspace in the UK and other countries, which are an invaluable resource to pilots and should always be checked before making a flight as they include any temporary restrictions which may be in force e.g. a Red Arrows flypast.

The CAA controls airspace in the UK, so permission is not required from owners of land and buildings to fly over their property although this must be done in a safe manner; in addition privacy issues could arise if you were, for example, to fly close to windows or hover over gardens or buildings for any length of time. Permission is required for takeoff and landing (TOAL) if this is to take place on privately-owned land.

While larger drones cannot generally be flown within 150m of built-up areas and 50m of people, there are no such minimum horizontal distance

The breakers' yards at Carlton, Barnsley, are well-known as the final resting place of many buses from all areas of Great Britain. While the Barnsley area was once home to numerous scrapyards, those at Carlton are now the only ones left which routinely cut buses. This aerial view taken on the afternoon of Saturday June 3, 2023, when the yards were closed, shows four separate scrapyards.

requirements for sub-250g drones which may even be flown over uninvolved people (defined as those not under the control of the drone pilot) although not over crowds.

My latest flying machine

The DJI Mini 3 Pro, which I acquired soon after release in May 2022, was the first drone to have a camera which could rotate to shoot in both landscape and portrait modes. Its lens is a 24mm wide angle (in 35mm full-frame equivalent focal length) with a fixed 1.7 aperture so is excellent for low-light and night photography.

I have six batteries, each of which gives a flight time of approximately 30min although this can be reduced depending on the type of flight. For example, if the drone is flown some distance to compose the image it will use more power than just hovering near to me, or it will use more power if it is flying into the wind.

The DJI Fly app, used to operate the drone, shows critical data such as height, distance and remaining battery power as well as warnings for high winds, obstacles and restricted zones. It has a return to home (RTH) function which allows it to return to the point from where it took off from although it can also be returned home manually, which I generally prefer.

As already mentioned, I previously owned the DJI Mavic Mini, followed by its successor the Mini 2, both of which were capable drones in terms of their photographic ability. However, the Mini 3 Pro is a vast improvement, the main advantage being that it has a larger sensor, allowing more detail to be captured.

It also has a burst-shooting mode of three, five or seven images which is a real advantage for fast-moving subjects such as buses or trains. I had found with the previous drones, which only shot a single frame, that sometimes a moving subject was not ideally placed in the frame as it is difficult to see things like road signs and other small objects on the live view so these could clash with the subject matter, detracting from the final composition. With a burst it is more likely that one of the frames will be perfectly-composed.

Mishap avoidance

The Mini 3 Pro also has obstacle avoidance sensors, which the previous Minis lacked. Although only on the front and underside, these reduce the likelihood of flying into trees or other obstacles; the drone will stop and hover if it senses an obstruction and corresponding warnings are provided on the app.

Unfortunately, not having rear sensors, it can still be flown backwards into things, as once happened with my Mini 2, which got caught in a bush on the bank of the Manchester Ship Canal when I was composing a picture of a ship, as I was distracted momentarily while talking to someone. Luckily, I retrieved the drone, miraculously free of any damage, by using the 'find my drone' function in the app which activates a beeper and flashing light on the drone and shows its position on a map. Five months later, I lost the same drone for good in the canal, again through my own negligence, but that is another story.

Since then I have been considerably more cautious when flying and ensure that nobody distracts me while I am operating the drone. I have had no further incidents and at the time of writing this, in June 2023, have undertaken 524 flights covering a combined distance of 265km and time of 68hr.

All the photographs in this feature were taken with the Mini 3 Pro, from RAW files processed in DxO Pure RAW, Adobe Photoshop and finally Nik Collection Color Efex Pro 4. With the latter, I mainly use the Pro Contrast filter to make the colours 'pop' and the neutral density graduated filter to lighten and/or darken the top and bottom areas of the image where necessary.

Using a drone has literally taken my photography to a different level. However, I can only see drone laws becoming more restrictive as time passes, even for the smaller drones, so will continue to make hay while the sun shines. ∎

The DJI Mini 3 Pro in flight.

A busy scene in Sheffield in April 2023 as buses turn into Commercial Street from Haymarket. Closely following a Stagecoach Yorkshire Alexander Dennis Enviro400 are a First South Yorkshire Volvo B9TL/Wright Eclipse Gemini 2 in yellow and red Mainline livery on the X78 from Doncaster and a Wright StreetLite Max on the cross-city 1a from Chapeltown to Herdings. A Stagecoach-operated Supertram is waiting at Fitzalan Square tram stop.

At the top of a steep cobbled road about 3miles north of Bury lies the tiny village of Nangreaves, one of the most isolated settlements in Greater Manchester. Originally served by Bury Corporation, which purchased two 20-seat Barnard-bodied Guy Wolfs in 1948 when a new service (49) was introduced, it is now served by Rosso's B2 Bury Bolts service. In March 2023, a short Alexander Dennis Enviro200 was there with traces of an earlier snowfall on the ground. It had left the turning circle at Mount Pleasant and was preparing to make a right turn into Walmersley Old Road to return to Bury. The red phone box now houses a heart defibrillator.

Built in the Brutalist architectural style and granted Grade II listed status in 2013, Preston Bus Station, opened in 1969, originally had 80 stands, 40 on each side, and was reputed to be the second largest in Western Europe. The stands on the east side were used principally by Ribble and Fishwick while Preston Corporation used those on the west side. All services now use the east side, with the west side turned into a public square as can be seen in this view as a Preston Bus Volvo B9TL with Wright Eclipse Gemini 2 body leaves in May 2023 on city service 8 to Moor Nook.

With branding for route 9 from Birmingham, an Alexander Dennis Enviro400 MMC of National Express West Midlands stands at Stourbridge Interchange in June 2023. The Interchange, with nine stands, was opened in 2012 on the site of an earlier bus station, which itself partly occupied the location of the original Stourbridge Town railway station, which was demolished in 1979 and the line cut back 70yd to make room for the bus station. At 0.8 miles long, the line from the replacement Stourbridge Town station to Stourbridge Junction is reputed to be the shortest operational branch line in Europe.

Pat Burnside's immaculate ECW-bodied Bristol SC4LK, new in January 1959, is the only fully-restored bus of this type in Tilling red. One of 78 purchased by Eastern Counties, LC556 looks perfectly at home in its Fenland surroundings as it crosses the Twenty Foot River at Beggar's Bridge, operating a service from Whittlesey to Turves, at the Fenland Busfest in May 2023.

The Shropshire town of Oswestry, 5miles from the Welsh border, changed hands between the two countries several times during the Middle Ages. In the 1860s it became the headquarters of the Cambrian Railways which built its works just north of the station and hastened Oswestry's boom as a railway town. The Grade II listed works is now a small business hub and antiques centre and is in this view. Tanat Valley Coaches, based in Llanrhaedr-Ym-Mochnant, in the extreme north of Powys, is now one of the principal operators in the town and three of its vehicles are in the layover bay outside the station. Nearest is a VDL SB180 with MCV Evolution body, behind is a VDL SB200 with Wright Pulsar 2 body and in the distance is a Mercedes-Benz Sprinter with Turkish-built Ilesbus i-City body. The Alexander-built Pacer train on the right is one of two operated by Cambrian Heritage Railways.

Operating service 410 from New Brighton to Clatterbridge Hospital in March 2023, a Wright Eclipse Gemini 2-bodied Volvo B5LH hybrid of Arriva North West crosses Duke Street Bridge, which joins the southern end of the Poulton district of Wallasey with the north end of Birkenhead. These are separated by the Great Float, a large body of water split into two large docks, East Float (to the right of the picture) and West Float (left of the bridge) which form part of Birkenhead Docks, now little-used by shipping. In its heyday the docks had their own railway system, which included a double-track line through this bridge.

Looking down on Newport Street, Bolton in May 2023 as a Wright StreetDeck of Diamond North West leaves the Interchange, partially visible on the right, on service 22 to the Trafford Centre. The earlier bridge over the railway line from Manchester to Wigan and Euxton Junction was replaced with this structure in 2006 featuring a 17m high arch. Bolton's equally distinctive Town Hall is piercing the skyline on the right.

A much busier port is Goole, on the River Ouse in the East Riding of Yorkshire. It is the UK's farthest inland port, being about 50miles from the North Sea. Passing along Bridge Street, which bisects the port, in June 2023 is one of two East Yorkshire Alexander Dennis Enviro200 MMCs with Goole Locals branding, operating service G1 from the town centre to Old Goole.

An Alexander Dennis Enviro200 in the Stagecoach Merseyside & South Lancashire fleet has just crossed the attractive Sutton Weaver swing bridge over the Weaver Navigation in April 2023 while operating service 2 from Palace Fields, Runcorn to Chester. Opened in 1926, the structure replaced an earlier swing bridge built in 1872. Until the 1990s, seagoing ships used the Navigation to reach Northwich, but it is now used only by leisure craft. Among the largest of these is the 1903-built Mersey Tug Daniel Adamson which is at her berth alongside the bridge.

Is this a **bus?**

PETER ROWLANDS shares his thoughts and pictures of some highly unusual vehicles he has photographed over the years, replicas, weird conversions, a van with a bus chassis and one that remains an unsolved mystery

Three young boys examine the Albany B Type replica in front of the old St Michael's Hospital (once a workhouse) in Enfield, close to the author's home in 1981. The radiator shell is squarer that those of real B Types.

I f you are anything like me, your archive of bus photographs will include a few pictures that you felt you had to take, though you never quite knew why: shots of replica buses, conversions and general oddball vehicles. They probably shouted 'I am a bus' at you – but not very persuasively.

Yet when I raided my collection in search of examples, I realised that most of them were just as fascinating as the conventional vehicles I usually photograph.

In some respects the most intriguing picture I found is one of a replica B Type double-decker. This was the model introduced by the London General Omnibus Company in 1910, then famously commandeered for troop transport in World War One. Several real examples survive, including B340, which is owned by the London Transport

Museum and has served as a template for various imitations over the years.

The replica that I photographed materialised one day in 1981, 50yd from my front door in Enfield, north London. I assumed when I embarked on this article that the internet would reveal a glorious history of its subsequent appearances at public events in the years since then, yet when I started my research it seemed to have vanished without trace.

It turns out that it was exported to the United States not long after I photographed it, and has remained there ever since. For some years it was based at the Crown Hotel in Inverness, Florida, about 65miles (105km) west of Orlando, but the hotel had mixed fortunes, and eventually the bus was acquired by the local council.

Its condition gradually deteriorated, and eventually it was sold for $1 to a private owner living in the area. The catch was that he was left with the task of restoring it, which was expected to cost up to $25,000. But he rose to the challenge, and the bus now gleams as brightly as when I photographed it.

It was one of two B Type replicas built by the Albany Motor Carriage Company of Christchurch, Dorset – a business founded in 1971 to produce veteran-style cars using modern drivetrains. Its other B Type, which was based on a Ford D-Series lorry chassis, is much better known. It was commissioned in the 1970s by Beaulieu Motor Museum in Hampshire, where it still gives visitors short rides to this day.

The vehicle in Florida also has Ford running units, though its body differs in many details from the Beaulieu example. In particular, it has a more square-cut radiator shell and bonnet line than its sibling, or indeed than any other B Types (real or replica) that I have been able to find. Its owner regularly gives it outings on parades and at other public events, and it spawned a fleet of CGI lookalikes when it made a cameo appearance in London scenes for the 2021 Disney movie *Jungle Cruise*, parts of which were filmed in Atlanta, Georgia.

Michelin's ersatz Schneider

Another replica evoking the same period was commissioned by Michelin in the early 1970s.

Michelin's Brillié Schneider replica bus was operating a shuttle service at the Tipcon tipper conference and exhibition in Harrogate in May 1978. Despite initial appearances, the three-cornered bracket on the front has no connection with Mercedes-Benz.

Knifeboard central seating was fitted on the top deck of Michelin's Brillié Schneider replica. Like many such vehicles, pneumatic tyres are a touch anachronistic even if they are more practical and comfortable than solid ones.

It recalls Paris double-deckers built in the early 1900s by French manufacturer Schneider. When new, these buses had a canopy above the upper deck that made them look immensely tall, but these were removed after a bus toppled over. The designer, Auguste Eugène Brillié, went on to develop what is thought to have been the first French battle tank, the Schneider CA1, in 1914.

The replica Brillié Schneider was built to support a programme of beach games organised by Michelin in the 1960s and 1970s. It was based on a Saviem chassis, with bodywork by Le Bastard de Rouen, which was famous for building outlandish promotional vehicles.

It was registered in France in June 1973, but went on to do sterling service in the UK in the 1970s and 1980s, appearing at fêtes, galas and other public events and at one Scottish Motor Show. I caught up with it in 1978 in Harrogate, where it was serving as a shuttle bus, ferrying delegates between venues at a Tipcon, a tipper lorry conference and exhibition hosted by the Road Haulage Association.

On the front of it was something that looked at a glance like a large Mercedes-Benz tri-cornered emblem, but the resemblance was coincidental. The original buses were fitted with Solex centrifugal syphon radiators produced by French engineering company Goudard & Mennenson, and this feature was simulated on the replica.

This immaculately turned-out Disney bus from the mid-1950s, believed to be the second example, was photographed in Disneyland in 1979.

Asquith's Transit-based buses gave a plausible impression of period vehicles. This one was rare in towing a trailer. It bore a cherished registration number reflecting the operator's name, Magpie Touring.

Mercedes-Benz had nothing to do with it. The bus still exists, and continues to be used by Michelin as a promotional vehicle.

Another bus that looks as if it dates from early last century is a double-decker that I photographed in Disneyland, California in 1979. It was one of a pair built by Disney in 1956/57 and put to work in the original Disney theme park. It is not based on any specific bus model, but makes a fair job of imitating vehicles of around 1910.

One of the two originals was moved to Disney's Epcot Center (Experimental Prototype Community of Tomorrow) in Florida in the early 1980s, and both have since been retired, but veteran-style double-deckers continue to run in Disney theme parks around the world. Later examples have been based on Ford chassis, but the originals are thought to

have been based on International petrol-engined chassis. Their bodywork was built by the Disney organisation itself.

A somewhat smaller replica bus that also imitated a type of vehicle rather than a specific model is one produced by Asquith Motors of Braintree, Essex. The company was founded in 1981 and offered a range of square-bonneted normal-control retro minibuses and vans based on Ford Transit chassis. More than a thousand of these were built before production tailed off around the turn of the century, and many were exported.

I photographed an example in Enfield in 1990 – this time a mile from my home. It was unusual in having a close-coupled trailer whose body was designed to align precisely with the vehicle itself. Its operator was called Magpie Touring.

The attempt at an exposed radiator on radically remodelled Bridgemaster 80 WMH bears little resemblance to those used on original AECs, and the relatively modern gasket-glazed windows undermine the attempt to create an inter-war look. Behind it is County Hall, still occupied by the Greater London Council in 1976.

Lower parts of the Bridgemaster's original back end were retained in the conversion, but the upper deck was cut short at the top of the staircase. Distantly in view across a remarkably quiet Westminster Bridge are the buildings that would be demolished in the late 1990s to make way for Portcullis House, the parliamentary overspill building.

In a later incarnation Asquith Motors still exists, and has plans to put several models from the old range back into production, as well as an electric version. Remarkably, its website includes a picture of the very vehicle and trailer I photographed over 30 years ago – presented as part of its current range. They was timeless then, so of course they are timeless still.

Bridgemaster taken back in time

One of the most bizarre retro vehicles I ever photographed was a double-decker bus converted in 1976 for Guards Coaches, London to look much older than it really was. It was based on 80 WMH, a Park Royal-bodied AEC Bridgemaster dating from 1959, but its concealed radiator had been rebuilt to look like an exposed radiator, and the staircase had been remodelled to evoke open-staircase buses of the 1920s.

In practice, the result was almost hilariously unconvincing. The radiator, although giving a nod to the famous AEC shell, was too wide and had an incorrect curved top, so it looked nothing like the real thing, though it did have an accurate replica AEC badge in the middle.

At the rear, the bus retained part of its original panelled flat back end rather than having a curving staircase, which would have been more typical of the buses it was trying to emulate. The upper-deck saloon had simply been cut away as far as the top of the existing staircase, leaving the stairs open to the elements. And the whole vehicle looked much too wide.

The original Bridgemaster had been used by AEC as a demonstrator, then spent most of its working life with independent operator Osborne's of Tollesbury, Essex. It had various non-standard features such as air suspension – an unlikely luxury on a genuine open-staircase bus. The Hanover Grand hospitality group, which owned Guards of London, used the vehicle to ferry tourists around central London to its West End attractions – notably The Cockney music hall in Charing Cross Road.

The conversion was done by Road Transport Services (Hackney) Ltd, a versatile company that usually focused on commercial vehicle bodybuilding. The company kept the main structure of the body intact, but cut off the front as well as the back of the upper deck, reducing seating capacity by seven altogether.

RTS did three more of these conversions for Guards, basing them on Leyland Titan PD3s formerly with Leicester City Transport. In due course Guards created a business unit called The Vintage Bus Company to run London sightseeing tours with these vehicles (no connection with the latter-day company of the same name).

After that, the Bridgemaster had yet another life. It was spotted in Antwerp in the mid-1990s, complete with Belgian registration plates and an attempt at an antique London General livery. It is thought to have appeared in at least one Continental feature film – giving a disappointingly inaccurate picture of past London buses.

London Transport's Supercar

If the conversion of the Bridgemaster was vigorous, the work done in 1991 on former London Transport Daimler Fleetline DMS1515 was nothing less than drastic. It was famously rebuilt to resemble a combined double-decker bus, Tube train and main line commuter train, and was named the Supercar. I spotted it in May 1992 in a park not far from where I lived.

The underlying bus dated from 1973. It had been retired prematurely in 1980, but had survived with London Transport as a training vehicle. The Supercar was created to promote One Day Travelcards, which had previously been known as Capitalcards, and was a joint venture between London Regional Transport, the successor to London Transport, and Network SouthEast, part of what was then British Rail.

The rebuilding was done by the people behind Pinefilms, which was based at Pinewood Studios and specialised in creating large sets for film productions. The Metro-Cammell Weymann body was cut off behind the first full window bay, and the door bay of a deep-level Tube train was fitted as the mid-section. The front of a Class 321 electric multiple unit became its back end.

Although it was not really intended for passenger use, authentic seating was provided in all sections, and it was possible to walk right through from front to back (or front to front). But there was no room for a staircase, so the upper deck of the front section was effectively a no-go area, though it did have seats.

At the front, the Supercar was pure London Transport Daimler Fleetline, but the body was cut short behind the front axle.

The rear engine of the Fleetline Supercar was cleverly encapsulated within the front end of a Class 321 electric multiple unit, creating this surreal look. Once parked, a pair of replica train wheels were fitted either side to hide the Fleetline's rear axle and the chassis parts behind.

Silver Cross operated more than a dozen of these pantechnicons based on Bristol LH bus chassis over the years. This Vanplan-bodied example is seen in Leicester in 1984.

The choice of vehicles for the three sections was a curious one. The Leyland-engined Fleetline was nearly 20 years old, and represented a class that had largely disappeared from the LRT fleet, though it had become popular with independents competing for tendered services in London. But it had been reviled by London Transport, which considered it under-specified for London operations.

Creating an eerie sense of push-me, pull-you, this Bedford TK's body features the roof and back windows of what is thought to be a Metro-Cammell bus body from the 1950s.

The British Rail section, by contrast, represented a new class of train that was still in the course of delivery, and would continue in service for more than 30 years. In a sense, the train section looked forward in time while the bus section looked back.

The Tube section fell somewhere between the two, representing a type that had been in service for over 20 years, and would continue for many years more. No doubt the assumption was that the travelling public would be unaware of the niceties of the different elements. The Supercar still exists, and can be seen from time to time at rallies.

These ones are lorries

My two final oddballs are not strictly buses at all, but lorries. One was operated by Silver Cross, a Yorkshire-based maker of prams, pushchairs and seating for high-performance cars. Between 1973 and 1983 the company bought more than a dozen delivery vans based on Bristol LH underfloor-engined bus chassis. This one was a long wheelbase LHL new in 1977.

The chassis suited the operation well because the underfloor engine gave the vehicles a low centre of gravity and even weight distribution – ideal for bulky but light loads such as prams. It also meant there was no engine tunnel in the cab to obstruct across access.

One could argue that this was not in any way a bus ... yet that Bristol LH badge on the front told a different story. This was a bus in disguise.

Marsdens of Warrington built the first few bodies, then the work was switched to Vanplan. Some bodies were transferred to newer chassis as the earlier ones were replaced. Marsden ended up acquiring Vanplan in 1986, but the combined company closed in 2005. Silver Cross is now part of a Chinese conglomerate.

My last photographic oddity is unmistakably a lorry – a Bedford TK with a 1977/78 registration – yet the roof and Luton head of its horsebox body have clearly been created from the roof and back end of a much older single-deck bus body. The rear route number indicator panel is still in place.

The effect is surreal. In the photograph the vehicle is coming towards the camera, yet the upper part of its body seems to be heading in the opposite direction. I took the picture in July 1988 in Elizabeth Street, Victoria, approaching Buckingham Palace Road.

I have to confess that I have been unable to find out anything about this vehicle. Why anyone would want to go to such lengths to create this bizarre body is a mystery. Our editor reckons the bus bodywork was probably built by Weymann in the 1950s, but if you know more about it, we would love to hear. ∎

Devon General
the **Western National** years

A reorganisation in 1971 by the National Bus Company placed Devon General, a former BET subsidiary, under the control of Western National which had been part of the state-owned Transport Holding Company. **ANDREW BABBS** recalls the gradual impact this had over the following years until it was all reversed in 1983

It appeared as if nothing had changed. The buses remained cherry red and ivory. They ran the same services, the route number had not altered, the timings were the same and on boarding the bus you would find the same driver or conductor collecting your fare. The crew continued to wear their smart Devon General uniform.

Come May 1971, when Devon General timetable number 167 came into operation, how many would have noticed that 'Omnibus & Touring Co. Ltd' was missing from the cover wording, or that inside the

front cover the same wording had been replaced with 'The Western National Omnibus Co. Ltd. Proprietors'? To a large degree, the larger concern treated the transfer of the Devon General business to Western National on New Year's Day 1971 as proprietorship.

Devon General operated as before albeit under the Western National legal entity. During the earlier years of the Western National proprietorship, barely into my teens, I spent a week each school Easter holiday riding round the network using a Go

Serving as a reminder of how Devon General still looked at the start of the 1970s is preserved Leyland Atlantean 872 recreating route 12 at Newton Abbot station in 2019 during a running day. It was new in 1959 and its 76-seat Metro-Cammell body has been restored to the cherry red and ivory livery it wore when BET owned the company. MARTIN CURTIS

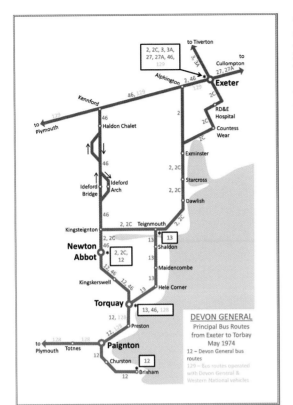

Map labels:

to Tiverton

2, 2C, 3, 3A, 27, 27A, 46, 129

to Cullompton 27, 27A

Alphington 2, 46

3, 3A

129

Exeter

46, 129

Kennford

2C

to Plymouth

129

129

RD&E Hospital

2C

46

Haldon Chalet

2

Countess Wear

2C

Exminster

46

2, 2C

Starcross

Ideford Bridge

Ideford Arch

2, 2C

Dawlish

46

2, 2C Teignmouth

2, 2C

Kingsteignton

2, 2C

13

*

13

Newton Abbot

46

Shaldon

2, 2C, 12

13

Kingskerswell

12, 46

12 46

13

Maidencombe

Hele Corner

Torquay

13

13, 46, 128

DEVON GENERAL

12, 128

Principal Bus Routes from Exeter to Torbay

12, 128

Preston

May 1974

to Plymouth

128

128

Paignton

12 – Devon General bus routes

Totnes

12

129 – Bus routes operated with Devon General & Western National vehicles

Churston

12

*

Brixham

12

Anywhere ticket. Towards the end of the Western National period I made numerous day and holiday visits to continue the acquaintance of the earlier years. What follow are my recollections from that era and the facets which interested this omnibologist.

Four forty-sixes

One of the early publicity campaigns to pass the eye, if not to come from the pen of Rick Hartnell, Western National group publicity manager, was that for Devon General route 46, the company's premier limited stop service linking Exeter, via the wooded roof of south Devon, with Newton Abbot and on via Kingskerswell to Torquay.

It employed three AEC Reliances, new in 1968 with Willowbrook bodies fitted with 49 coach-type seats. Not that anyone would realise they were other than ordinary buses (unless they travelled on them), for they wore bus livery.

Whether it was contrived or a great coincidence, in 1971 the public was exhorted to 'Ride on bus number 46 on service 46, offering a round trip of 46 miles at 46p return'. And to ensure you knew which was bus 46 (and 45 and 47), the trio were re-liveried in ivory with cherry red window surrounds – a single-deck

equivalent of the livery carried by the Seadog-class open-top Leyland Atlanteans. The purpose of the publicity was to draw attention to the step-up to an hourly summer frequency from Monday July 5.

The first time I used the 46 it was simply as a quick way for a 13-year-old to get from Exeter to Torquay. I had 5hr to do a round trip if I was to arrive back at Brushford Cross on time in the early evening and thus avoid parental ire. So the flash livery and comfortable seats, while welcome, were not the prime reasons for making the trip. That was to see the hordes of Atlanteans abounding in Torquay, for Exeter only had a few – mainly on the Rifford Road circular route R.

I was glad the driver of the 12:00 departure from Exeter knew his way out of the city on to the A38 as on this, and many subsequent trips, I never fathomed it out for myself. We got moving reasonably well once on the dual-carriageway to Kennford. Then came the completely unexpected – Haldon Hill – at the time a mire of roadworks. We took the A380 towards Newton Abbot and the Reliance chugged its way up. I thought I could have walked up faster but stayed on board and counted the cats' eyes as each one passed. Once up top, we got going again.

It was fascinating how the A380 split into an old and new carriageway, one for each direction. Ideford Arch was served southbound – we stopped there – while northbound on the newer road it is Ideford Bridge at the bottom of a dip. Newton Abbot bus station was a brief halt before the classy Reliance was off again.

It was spot-the-Atlantean time thence into Torquay as they passed the other way on busy route 12. The 46's Torquay terminus was a revelation: Torwood Street Grey Cars coach station. I had never seen so many Grey Cars all together before. I walked up and down noting down the numbers, paying especial attention to the E-registered examples as they were not in the Ian Allan *British Bus Fleets 8*. What I missed that day was the second lower deck of the coach station accessed from the street round the back. Beginner's luck.

But I did get an Atlantean ride that day, on a 13 to Teignmouth, before riding an AEC Regent on the 2 to get me back to Exeter within the allotted 5hr

Fleet numbering

At the close of 1970 the Devon General fleet comprised single-deck buses and coaches numbered from 1 to 87, double-deckers in the range 501-41, a mixture of all types in the earlier series up to 991, plus the former City of Exeter fleet in the 200s.

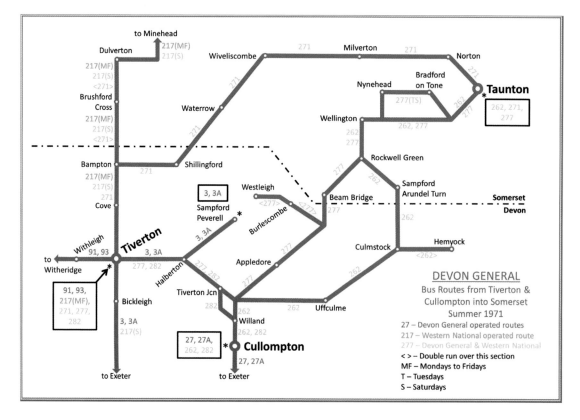

DEVON GENERAL
Bus Routes from Tiverton &
Cullompton into Somerset
Summer 1971
27 – Devon General operated routes
217 – Western National operated route
277 – Devon General & Western National
< > – Double run over this section
MF – Mondays to Fridays
T – Tuesdays
S – Saturdays

It has always surprised me that none needed to be renumbered when combined into the Western National fleet and neither did any Western National vehicles. Such a neat merger of the two series did not happen overnight. It had clearly been foreseen by the engineering team at Western National with careful allocation of new fleetnumbers – even to the extent of changing the Bristol LHs, with 1564 upwards following 750-63 to avoid getting too close to Devon General's earlier series.

New Devon General vehicles were added to the existing series up to 1978, with single-deckers being 88-93, then 100 upwards for Bristol LHs, and new Bristol VRTs were 542 onwards.

A separate series for new Grey Cars coaches had been planned to start at 450 following Western National's Bristol SUL coaches numbered 400-33. Even some new dual-door Bristol RELLs and Leyland Nationals, ostensibly for the Exeter fleet, were numbered 225-9 and 230-5 respectively. Eventually the illusion that a separate Devon General fleet existed was discontinued and all new vehicles were added to Western National number blocks irrespective of their colour or fleetname.

Devon General in Somerset

For much of its existence, Devon General had operated principally within the well-populated areas surrounding Exeter and Torbay. One exception was the long south coast route into Dorset from Exeter run jointly with Southern National. By 1970 this had become Devon General to Axminster, change to Western National for Weymouth. Similarly, the once joint route to Minehead had become a change to Western National at Tiverton. Reasonably timed connections were available at both locations.

In north-east Devon, Western National had a small network based on Tiverton and Cullompton, linking the two towns and serving the surrounding area. Western National kept buses for these services locally at an outstation. Western National also operated routes 271 and 277, connecting Dulverton and Tiverton respectively with Taunton.

One early result of making the Devon General legal entity the same as that of Western National was the combination of the two concerns' Tiverton operations under the Devon General banner. Two of Tiverton's Western National drivers joined the Devon General team, and Devon General drivers began route learning on the 271 and 277. The 271

Andrew Babbs's trip back from Taunton to Brushford Cross in spring 1971 was on a Marshall-bodied AEC Reliance of the same batch as 73 (OTA73G), photographed a few years later in NBC poppy red but still with chrome brightwork around the front and back. Tiverton had a large allocation of these well regarded vehicles.

gained some Dulverton-Bampton-Tiverton trips to enable operation from both ends.

Picking up on these route changes in an amendment booklet to the 1970 Devon General timetable, I took a day out to Taunton, outward by the 277 and back by the 271. My day began early at Brushford Cross, on the 07:00 trip down the Exe valley to Tiverton. Following what seemed like an inordinately long wait at Phoenix Lane, I set off for Taunton on the 277 on a Western National vehicle which I think was a Bristol RE. Far from being a quick dash up the A38, this diverted into and through small villages on the way.

At the end of the day, I took the 271 back from Taunton to Brushford Cross – and on this journey I enjoyed the superior ambience of one of Devon General's OTA-G AEC Reliances. The 271 was a direct route staying on the A361 all the way to Bampton. I remained aboard for the trip up to Dulverton before alighting at Brushford Cross on the return southwards, thus riding the complete route.

The quintessential THC fleet

Even before Devon General became part of Western National in 1971, new vehicle policy and ordering was being managed from National House, Exeter.

So, at a stroke, the vehicle orders took on a distinct Transport Holding Company flavour.

If there was a surprise, it was that Western National switched to Plaxton to body its coaches. Hence the new vehicles expected by Devon General for 1971 were almost a mirror image of the Western National types – Bristol LHS buses, Bristol VRT double-deckers and Plaxton Panorama Elite-bodied Bristol RELH coaches for Grey Cars. The only vehicles with a BET ring about them were the final seven Leyland Panthers which had been ordered by City of Exeter with BET-style bodies by Marshall. All the buses duly arrived in Devon General cherry red and ivory. Deliveries throughout the rest of the 1970s wore National Bus Company poppy red but 1980s arrivals were leaf green and, on some examples, with Western National fleetnames.

It was not only the 'new' fleet which bore the THC hallmark, as used vehicles did too. First in were ten Bristol SUL4As, ECW-bodied of course, which saw off the similarly-engined Albion Nimbuses. They might have looked smart in poppy red but had no one in the engineering team at National House compared their basic interiors to the infinitely superior accommodation that Devon General had deemed was appropriate for passengers?

Among the Western National vehicles cascaded to Devon General were several ECW-bodied Bristol MW6G coaches like 2982 (EDV 503D) with rebuilt front destination display and painted in local coach livery. Retention of coach seating enabled their continued occasional use on National Express work, as here seen in Exeter Coach Station in April 1977.

A later programme of re-casting Royal Blue's Bristol MW coaches for a life in the bus world kept the coach seating. Those allocated to Devon General looked extremely smart in poppy red and white livery applied in local coach style.

The strangest additions to the Devon General fleet were two Bristol Lodekka FSFs — 1012/13 (707/8 JHY) — transferred from Western National and repainted poppy red; they had been new to Bristol Omnibus Company and had come to Western National in 1967 in lieu of new Lodekka FLFs which had been diverted to Bristol. They ran on Exeter-Newton Abbot routes 186/187 alongside the Exe and Teign estuaries with views of the sea in between, supporting AEC Regents.

With a mature service network and the regulatory system of the 1930s, there was

AEC Regent V 512 (CTT 512C) with highbridge Park Royal body alongside one of the two Bristol Lodekka FSFs, 1012 (707 JHY) new to Bath Tramways in 1960, in Belgrave Road garage yard, Exeter in April 1977. Both their destination displays are for route 187, successor to the 2C.

little scope to offer new connections to benefit passengers. Most service alterations were reductions to match resources to passenger numbers. Plus there was the cull of unremunerative routes in 1971, although Devon General suffered fewer outright withdrawals than other parts of Western National.

On the positive side ,new facilities were offered. Half of service 2 (Newton Abbot-Exeter) was re-routed on the approach to the city, as route 2C, to cross the River Exe by the original Exeter bypass to Countess Wear roundabout, then ran in via Topsham Road to stop close by the Royal Devon & Exeter Hospital at Barrack Road.

This was a popular move, for by 1976 when the Devon General routes were renumbered for 12 months, the majority of the service ran this way as the 187, leaving only a few peak-hour 186 trips along the original route via Alphington. The route continued with operation by large front-entrance Regents, supported by the FSFs.

Grant coaches
When the National Bus Company announced its orders for new vehicles for 1974, Western National's included eight Bristol RELH with Plaxton coach bodies.

This puzzled me at the time, as there was also an order for 17 apparently similar coaches. Why not simply 25? When they began to arrive from Plaxton the reason for the distinction became clear. Devon General was getting the eight, which came in two pairs of four, painted in poppy red and white local coach livery. The first, 2500-3 (PUO 500-3M), arrived in summer 1974 and replaced the AEC Reliances on the

46 Express, and also took over some duties on the 129 Exeter-Plymouth service. These had Gardner engines.

Arriving early 1975 with Leyland engines and among the last RELHs constructed, were 2504-7 (GFJ 670-3N), to upgrade the passenger comfort on the 128 Torquay-Plymouth route. On a journey on the 46 to Torquay in spring 1975, I noted that the performance of the RELH up Haldon Hill was superior to that of the replaced Reliances though still taxing on the Gardner engine. But what luxury to be travelling by coach, even though it had two-piece bus grant doors.

Route renumbering
It was all change up front in the route number section of Devon General buses' destination displays in 1975. Numbers used for the entire life of Devon General, and etched indelibly in the travelling public's memory, were jettisoned, replaced by numbers in the Western National series of 1xx for Torbay & south Devon and 3xx for east and mid-Devon.

The new system did away with the suffix letters used by Devon General to denote route variations which resulted in some then running under the main number. Perhaps computerisation triggered the change to avoid confusion between two identically numbered routes, but although there were two 93s in the Devon General timetable book, folk in Tiverton waiting to catch a 93 to Witheridge would not get confused because the Western National 93 left Dartmouth 10min later for Kingsbridge.

The approach to renumbering varied greatly between the 1xx and 3xx series. In Torbay there

Area	New route numbers	Comment
Paignton and Brixham	100s and 110s	Included Western National Paignton routes
Torquay	120s, 130s, 140s, 150s and 160	Also 128 (Torquay-Plymouth) and 129 (Exeter-Plymouth)
Totnes	160s	Mainly Western National routes
Newton Abbot	170s, 180s and 190s	
Exmouth and Sidmouth	330-342, 356-358, 371	
Tiverton	344-355	
South-west of Exeter	359-360, 364-366, 370, 372	Devon General 46 Express became 370
Cullompton	361-363, 378-379	
Cowley Bridge and Crediton	367-369, 376-377	
Honiton and Axminster	375, 380-382	
Okehampton	383, 384	

was a progression of number blocks south to north with all but five routes gaining new numbers. Where adding 100 to the number placed it in the correct number block this was done.

Various tactics were employed in east and mid-Devon: adding 300, 320 or 340 to the Devon General number, numbering some interurban services immediately adjacent to these, employing two area number blocks and another for some interurban routes, and ad hoc renumbering of the remainder. It was all a bit messy.

Escaping renumbering were Devon General's Paignton circulars 104/105, a works service numbered 126 and the 'jointly-operated' 128/129 linking Plymouth with Torquay and Exeter. Exeter city services retained their route letters.

Timetables

Having a timetable was essential to plan a day's outing using a Go-Anywhere ticket. It also came in handy to revise my itinerary if something went awry while travelling. The first Devon General timetable

I purchased was sent for by post, with a postal order to cover the cost, and duly arrived from National House, Exeter. It was Devon General issue 166, valid May 1970 to May 1971. As things turned out it was the last timetable the company produced.

Unlike earlier issues, its cover was in the new NBC corporate style with the top part white and the lower part, with an outline map of the area served, in an approximation of cherry red. Printing was by Wheaton of Exeter. Five further similar looking issues were produced under the Western National proprietorship, the deep red being changed to a much lighter shade (poppy red?) from the 1973 edition. The last, in 1975, contained all the familiar services in a totally different order according to the new route numbers.

From 1976 to 1980, an all-Devon timetable was issued annually, covering Devon General and Western National services with a section on independent offerings funded by Devon County Council. From 1981 it was replaced by thinner volumes covering the Exeter area (services in the

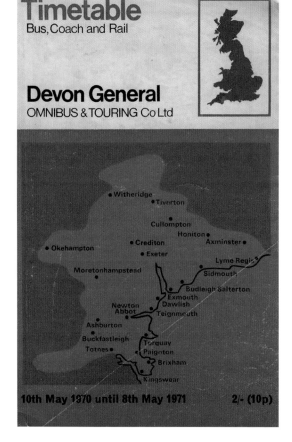

A contrast in timetable designs between 1970 and 1981. The 1970 cover price of 10p is equivalent of £1.30 today and 25p in 1980 is around 90p today.

The livery of the two Willowbrook 003-bodied Leyland Leopards selected for the X38 Exeter-Plymouth express seemed something of a paradox: a deep, poppy red band on the body sides married with Western National fleetnames. Despite one coach being based in each terminal city, neither carried the Devon General title. This view of 3537 (FDV 828V) in Exeter Bus Station shows the good made use of the boot door to advertise the service.

300s) and Torbay and South Devon (the 100s). The covers were a little plain on the first Torbay issues, but both coalesced after that into a rather attractive style with coloured border surrounding an ink sketch of an easily identified street scene in which ECW-bodied Bristol VRs went about their business.

The first phase of deregulation, from October 6, 1980, brought the new two-hourly X38 Exeter-Plymouth express stopping only at Drumbridges roundabout, the A38 junction for Bovey Tracey. Recently delivered Leyland Leopards with Willowbrook 003 grant coach bodies were employed, painted white with a broad poppy red band and prominent route decals.

The relaxed road service licensing rules also led to a makeover of service 370 (Exeter-Torquay) as the X80 from January 17, 1982. It was re-routed via the Royal Devon & Exeter Hospital, just as service 2C had been ten years earlier, and extended beyond Torquay to Paignton. Leopard grant coaches gained a similar livery to those on the X38, but with X80 branding.

It's Devon General again
Running all the buses in four large counties in the west of England from National House in Exeter

fitted with NBC policy at the time as it assimilated former BET and THC under one umbrella.

One thing that stood out in this process was the retention of Devon General as a trading name alongside Western National. It even kept a red livery until the early 1980s. And while its replacement with leaf green seemed to be the next step towards complete integration, NBC policy was changing.

Before the fleetname itself was dropped and while some buses remained red, Western National was split into four smaller units, each a company in its own right. So Devon General was reborn on January 1, 1983 and poppy red returned. It was not the Devon General Omnibus & Touring Company reinvigorated, but a new Devon General Ltd.

For a year there was little change. The new vehicles ordered by Western National arrived, fleetnumbers remained as planned by Western National and timetable books were largely identical to the Western National creations of 1981 onwards. But it was soon clear that Devon General's Western National years were over as changes wrought by the new management in Exeter to increase frequencies on urban services would reverberate around Britain. ■

Drew's old masters

CHRIS DREW takes us into an art gallery of his imagination to view some of his favourite bus and tram photographs as framed works of art

Regal Entrance

Regal Entrance

Master of the country lane
Devon General 487
at a Kingsbridge Running Day
c. 2019

New Reflecting the Old
Glass reflecting stone in Nottingham
with Trent Barton Volvo
in between
c. 2010

New Reflecting the Old

Family Portrait

A Family Portrait
Celebrating
100 Years of the
East Kent Road Car Co.
at Herne Bay
c.2016

Not Quite Narnia

Not quite Narnia
(with reference to the lamp post)
Anglian Mercedes at
Aldburgh
c. 2009

Last one out...
..please turn off the lights
late night wash of a
Dennis Dart at Sheerness
c. 2010

Last one out...

Flemish Grand Master
Van Hool 4272
carefully picks its way
along Spiegelrei by the canal
in Bruges
c. 2013

Flemish Grand Master

AH VIENNA

Ah Vienna
Duewag GT SGP
type E2 tram
number 4026
heading for Nassdorf
c. 2018

One of the last secondhand double-deckers that the original McGill's bought was JXC 201, one of 74 of London Transport's prematurely sold Cravens-bodied RT-class AEC Regent IIIs sold to Scottish operators. The former RT1438 was one of five that Garelochhead Coach Services purchased straight out of London service in 1956 and McGill's bought it four years later and sold it for scrap in 1969. This picture was taken in Renfrew in May 1962 when it was in the company of two of the other local independents' vehicles, an ex-Bury Corporation Massey-bodied Leyland Titan TD5 with Paton's of Renfrew and a Burlingham Seagull-bodied Leyland Royal Tiger coach with Garner's of Bridge of Weir. IAIN MacGREGOR

McGill's
A name that was reborn

Today's McGill's group, with operations across central Scotland, has its origin in a 20-vehicle independent with a small but prominent presence in the eastern part of Renfrewshire from the 1930s to the 1990s

The McGill's group today is the largest family-owned independent operator in Scotland, with nearly 700 vehicles at seven depots across the centre of the country, from Greenock in the west to Livingston and Dundee in the east.

The Easdale family, brothers James and Sandy, have built it up since acquiring control of it in 2004

but its name — McGill's Bus Service — comes from something much smaller, a business founded and run by three generations of the McGill family for over 60 years from the town of Barrhead in eastern Renfrewshire, the last of the pre-deregulation independents serving Paisley and its adjoining communities. An operator with the air of a small municipal undertaking that Iain MacGregor, who lived and worked in the area, followed closely and photographed frequently

James McGill's first venture into bus operation began over 100 years ago, in 1921, when he established his Carrick Pullman Service in the village of Crosshill in rural south Ayrshire, providing a scheduled service into the county town of Ayr. He sold it in September 1932 to the recently created Western SMT company and in November the following year moved north to Barrhead to acquire a business called J O'Hara & Company which operated five single-deck Albions between Barrhead and nearby Paisley.

McGill's introduced its first double-deckers from 1940 and secured road service licences to add two more routes in the 1950s, partly to replace Glasgow Corporation trams when they were withdrawn from Paisley, Renfrew and Barrhead in 1957. Against stiff opposition from Strathclyde PTE, it fought and won another battle in the early 1980s to establish a new route between Barrhead and Glasgow city centre. It also owned a separate business, Rothesay Motor Services, on the Isle of Bute from 1955 until it sold those services to Western SMT in 1965.

By 1972, Duple Midland-bodied Ford Thames TOO 557 was McGill's only single-decker. It was nearly 18 months old when bought from Ford's demonstration fleet in 1964 and ran initially for the Rothesay subsidiary. IAIN MacGREGOR

Management of the company passed from James to Frank McGill in the late 1950s and to his son Gordon McGill in the 1980s.

New vehicles to the fore
It bought its first new bus (an Albion) in 1935 and its first new double-deckers (utility Guy Arabs) in 1944 and although it continued to purchase some

McGill's first new double-deckers were four Guy Arab II utilities supplied in 1944/45 with Park Royal bodies. All four were rebodied by Massey in 1955 and Gardner 5LW-engined CHS 271 outlived the other three, not being sold until 1972. It still looked smart, its chassis then almost 26 years old, when photographed in Paisley in April 1970. IAIN MacGREGOR

Six new Leyland Titans with Leyland's own body design (the first of them was built by Alexander) were delivered between 1947 and 1954. The last of them, GHS 994, was a PD2/12 with the final body design with radiused windows which remained in the fleet until 1969. By the time this picture was taken in Paisley in July 1964, McGill's had dropped maroon from its livery. IAIN MacGREGOR

McGill's changed its allegiance from Leyland to Daimler in 1960 with the purchase of two Massey-bodied CVG6s which, unusually, in 1974 were sold for further service with one of the members of the A1 Service cooperative in Ayrshire. This shows OHS 980 in Paisley in September 1971. IAIN MacGREGOR

secondhand, its last such double-decker was an ex-demonstrator in 1961. New double-deckers predominated, with 23 purchased between 1947 and 1973. Protracted delays in the delivery of new Daimler Fleetlines hastened a decision to switch to single-deckers and standardise on the Leyland National from 1977 until the end of production nine years later. Its final purchases were of new step-entrance Dennis Darts.

It became the first Scottish company to operate articulated buses — bendybuses — in 1983 when it acquired two 60-seat three-year-old Leyland-DABs ex-South Yorkshire PTE to operate the Glasgow service.

The company's presence was reinforced in the area by a smart livery of red, maroon and grey until 1964 when it was simplified by discontinuing the use of maroon. It changed its fleetname in the 1960s from a crescent-like scroll into a fully spelt-out name that left no doubt of the company's identity or the locality in which it was based. The scroll name reappeared in the 1980s.

Although regulation made it hard for operators like McGill's to win traffic court battles, road

The third Daimler double-decker was VKV 99, a Willowbrook-bodied CVG6LX-30 that was a Daimler demonstrator from 1958 until it joined the McGill's fleet in March 1961. It was withdrawn towards the end of 1978. IAIN MacGREGOR

service licensing also protected them from predatory competition. That comfort ended with deregulation in October 1986 when McGill's and the other surviving Paisley independent, Graham's Bus Service, came under pressure from new minibus operators on their routes that forced them to compete to survive. Graham's lasted only until

McGill's embraced rear engines with 14 Daimler Fleetlines bought new between 1963 and 1973. The first had Northern Counties coachwork but Alexander bodied the others. The final four had Gardner 6LXB engines and lowheight bodies to Scottish Bus Group specification. NHS 782L, photographed in April 1978, was one of the last pair. More Fleetlines were ordered but cancelled as delivery dates kept being delayed. IAIN MacGREGOR

Alexander-bodied Fleetlines included two delivered in 1970 which the coachbuilder persuaded the company to take as extras on a run of Leyland Atlanteans for Edinburgh Corporation with two doors and panoramic windows. This 1974 view shows XHS 923H in Barrhead. IAIN MacGREGOR

Structural problems led to the two dual-door Fleetlines being rebuilt in 1977 in the Greater Glasgow PTE workshops. The centre doors (unnecessary in a business that still employed conductors) were removed and short windows were installed in the lower deck. This is XHS 924H. IAIN MacGREGOR

XYS 595S was the third of 14 Leyland Nationals bought new. It was exhibited at the Scottish Motor Show in November 1977 and entered service early in 1978 with a crest marking Queen Elizabeth II's silver jubilee in 1977. IAIN MacGREGOR

April 1990 but McGill's soldiered on and expanded westwards in 1995 to the town of Johnstone and the village of Kilbarchan in competition with Clydeside, the privatised successor to the northern part of Western SMT.

It finally admitted defeat in July 1997, selling out to the Cowie group which by then already owned Clydeside and which renamed itself Arriva later in the year. It maintained McGill's separate identity until 1999 when it was subsumed into what by then was Arriva Scotland West. Its surviving buses were soon repainted in corporate aquamarine and Cotswold stone. The events of 1932 seemed to have repeated themselves. McGill's would be no more. Apparently.

The new McGill's is born
Except that Arriva was at the start of its complete exodus from Scotland. Under competitive attack from more of the new generation of independents with small vehicles, the Scotland West operations in the Inverclyde towns of Greenock, Port Glasgow and Gourock were performing badly and in June 2001 they were sold to one of the new

entrepreneurs, a businessman called Alex Kean who announced that his new venture would trade as Greenock & District Omnibuses.

However, rather than set up a shelf company to effect this transaction, Arriva — which had already concluded that the McGill's name was

FHE 292V, one of two Leyland-DAB bendybuses with Leyland National bodywork that were acquired ex-South Yorkshire PTE, in Glasgow city centre in August 1983. McGill's red and grey stripes replaced orange and green ones in the South Yorkshire livery. IAIN MacGREGOR

N439 GHG, a Dennis Dart with Northern Counties Paladin body, in Johnstone in 1996. IAIN MacGREGOR

of no value to it — revived the dormant McGill's Bus Service limited company and sold it to Kean along with its operator licence and the registered services in Inverclyde. And thus it was, with a royal blue and white livery, that the new owner chose to trade as McGill's instead of the planned geographical title.

The new McGill's relocated from the Arriva depot in Greenock to premises owned by the Easdales, whose wider business interests include a substantial property portfolio. The Easdales acquired full ownership in October 2004 and the business expanded westwards in 2008 to establish services in the Paisley area and to occupy the old McGill's depot in Barrhead which Arriva had closed six years earlier.

Rapid expansion followed, as McGill's acquired most of the new age independents in the area who would otherwise have struggled to comply with minimum vehicle standards enshrined in a statutory quality partnership with Strathclyde Partnership for Transport, the restructured former PTE. But a far bigger leap forward came in March 2012 when McGill's bought the remainder of Arriva Scotland West with its Paisley area depots at Inchinnan and Johnstone.

A national and cross-border operator

Subsequent expansion east of Glasgow to acquire small operators in North Lanarkshire was less successful, but two further retreats by big groups have transformed the group into something much larger. National Express Group sold its Xplore Dundee business — the former municipal undertaking in Scotland's fourth largest city — to McGill's in January 2021.

McGill's followed that in September 2022 with the last remnants of First Scotland East, with the fleet at its Bannockburn, Larbert and Balfron depots in Stirlingshire rebranded as Midland Bluebird, while bus operations at Livingston in West Lothian became Eastern Scottish, both of these being identities first used by the Scottish Bus Group. Livingston also is the base for Bright Bus Tours, an open-top sightseeing operation in Edinburgh that First launched in 2019 in competition with Lothian Buses' Edinburgh Bus Tours subsidiary.

McGill's entered into a partnership with Flixbus in July 2021, operating overnight and daytime coach services for the German-owned giant. By summer 2023 these linked major Scottish cities with London and several other English cities and competed with Scottish Citylink within Scotland. ∎

The McGill's fleet in Renfrewshire has taken delivery of 96 Yutong E12 and E10 battery-electric single-deckers. I5012 (SG71 MXU) is an E12 operated from the former Arriva depot at Inchinnan. ALAN MILLAR

The latest Eastern Scottish livery on 8961 (YX62 BPU), an Alexander Dennis Enviro400 new to First London. KEITH McGILLIVRAY

Midland Bluebird 0448 (SN64 CJZ), a Wright StreetLite DF acquired with the First Scotland East business. DAVID OAKLEY

You had to be there

Local registration marks helped identify a vehicle's origin in past decades, but there were things that that defied written descriptions, as **ROGER DAVIES** recalls, like the livery, destination display and how the fleetnumbers were applied, if at all. There was no substitute for going to see them in the metal.

An interest in buses can go much farther than just the vehicles themselves. I am constantly amazed by the incredible depth of knowledge on fairly obscure subjects that can be found. It is this broadness of interest, coupled with the fact the industry is so dependent on people, that makes it such an absorbing pastime. Some aspects have gone, others remain, but here are some thoughts on the subject

My fascination with buses goes back a long way, longer than I remember. I have notebooks where, in my own hand, are the registrations of Cardiff Corporation buses I do not remember seeing. By the time I could check them, my fascination having turned into hobby, interest and finally a career, and they were long gone. Wartime Bristols they were, and by the time I became more aware they were

driver trainers, a tower wagon and a quaint halfcab flatbed truck for shifting trolleybus poles around the place.

The first point here is registrations. I did not note nor likely see fleetnumbers. The latter could be changed but, mostly, the registration stayed with the bus for its life. This made identification after sale a great deal easier if the bus went on to other things,.

And it gave strong local identity as, until the early 1970s, registration offices were very local affairs. Thus, most municipals, and when I became a serious bus enthusiast there were 97 of them, could be identified by the registrations issued by the local authorities that owned them. For me in south Wales this meant Cardiff buses were BO, KG or UH, Newport DW and Merthyr HB. This was a further part of local identification of buses. Swansea did not have its own buses, but as near as makes no

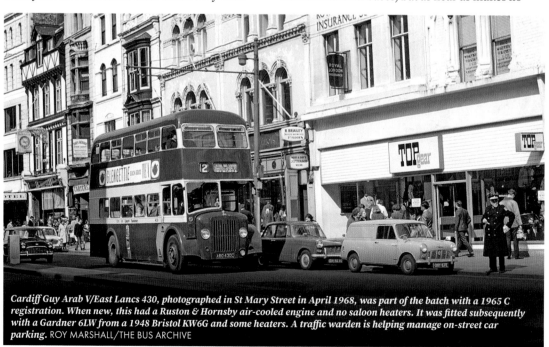

Cardiff Guy Arab V/East Lancs 430, photographed in St Mary Street in April 1968, was part of the batch with a 1965 C registration. When new, this had a Ruston & Hornsby air-cooled engine and no saloon heaters. It was fitted subsequently with a Gardner 6LW from a 1948 Bristol KW6G and some heaters. A traffic warden is helping manage on-street car parking. ROY MARSHALL/THE BUS ARCHIVE

difference, it had South Wales Transport ones with the local CY and WN registrations.

Some municipals, however, served areas too small to have their own registrations, so used ones issued by the county they were in which, while losing localness, gave them a sort of other worldly appeal. Aberdare, Bedwas & Machen, Caerphilly, Gelligaer and Pontypridd all used Glamorgan's NY, TG and TX. West Monmouthshire across the border in that county sported its AX and WO. Even better endowed Lancashire could easily match this variety. Of course, this made subsequent identification a bit tricky, but not a lot of that happened

A bigger challenge

Company operators were more of a challenge. They largely registered their buses where their head office was. So Western Welsh had Cardiff registrations, Trent Derby and Southdown Brighton. As many company buses did go on for further service, the registration gave you a clue how to track it down. There were some pitfalls, if a very big company was registered where there was a much smaller municipal, it could trap the unwary. I have seen various ex-Preston Corporation buses erroneously claimed as Ribble.

Again, if the head office was somewhere that did not have its own registrations, the local county was used like West Yorkshire Road Car in Harrogate.

There was one unusual fleet. The huge Midland Red covering a vast area including a big presence in Birmingham had its head office in Solihull, so used its one registration, HA, for all its buses, Movement of a head office would affect this. Neath & Cardiff moved out of Swansea to Briton Ferry, so from 1965 its coaches were registered in Glamorgan. An unusual situation was the Northern General group. Each constituent fleet had its own head office and registered its buses locally, giving an interesting mix.

Scotland managed to corner all the registrations with S in them, but had more with other letter. Glasgow's haul had GD and famously had over 700 vehicles registered SGD. It also used all 999 of FYS and Birmingham used all of JOJ too, which meant both fleets had buses with registrations from many years prior to their building, That was an odd thing to do and Western National had some similar and more complex fun with LTA.

London had loads. I could never quite understand it, but it was interesting how the first four groups of Routemasters had LT plates. There were nice oddities like the Isle of Man with MAN, Jersey with J and Guernsey with just numbers. Northern Ireland had its own series, which using letters such as Z omitted elsewhere gave them a distinct individuality.

When the series with letters in front ran out, it was simply reversed but not all places followed the same

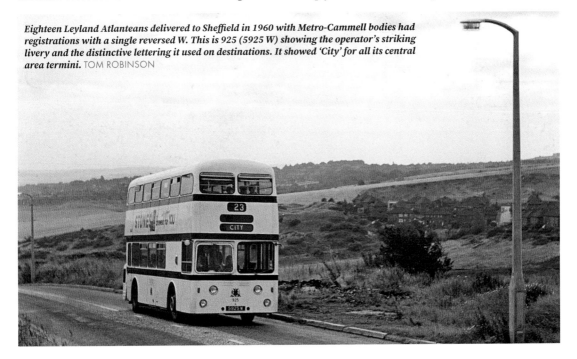

Eighteen Leyland Atlanteans delivered to Sheffield in 1960 with Metro-Cammell bodies had registrations with a single reversed W. This is 925 (5925 W) showing the operator's striking livery and the distinctive lettering it used on destinations. It showed 'City' for all its central area termini. TOM ROBINSON

The National Bus Company got rid of the hugely popular Neath & Cardiff brand and absorbed it into mainly South Wales with a bit going to Western Welsh. In anticipation, the 1970 delivery of two Plaxton-bodied AEC Reliances had Derwent bus shells rather than Panorama Elite coach, a premonition of it becoming just any other bus service. Also these two reverted to Swansea registrations. Then new UCY 980J shows this pair's unique service description above the windscreen and the stunning livery no words in a fleetlist could convey. Port Talbot steelworks is in the background. GEOFFREY MORANT

line. Some, like Sheffield, went back to the original single or two letters but most carried on with three.

It was realised that this system would run out and some places were coming near that. So a new system of year suffix started in 1963 and for four years was eminently sensible, telling you when the vehicle was first registered. From 1967, giving in to car salesmen, the changeover date was moved to August and from 1999 to twice a year, in March and September, making it all a bit pointless.

But it did bring yet another facet to bus enthusiasm. In January 1965, I was walking home from school along St Fagans Road in Cardiff when a shiny new bus approached. At the time, City of Cardiff Transport was taking in 12 short East Lancs-bodied Guy Arab Vs, five long ones having been delivered some months previously. They were allocated the first suffix registrations, ABO-B with matching numbers. Delivery of the short ones was fitful, only three, 431/3/4, having materialised in 1964. The one that approached me was the fourth, 426 and it was boldly registered ABO 426C. I was beside myself with excitement.

Such things became the norm thereafter, Western Welsh managing registration of some Park Royal-bodied Leyland Tiger Cubs a year later where the first half dozen had FUH-C registrations on the odd numbers and FUH-D on the evens. But it was not universal. As East Lancs was sending those Arab Vs to Cardiff, it was also sending AEC Regent Vs to Southampton. B registrations with matching numbers went on those arriving in 1964, but those coming in 1965 had totally different C registrations with non-matching numbers. Why on earth was that?

Matching numbers
Many operators did match fleet and registration numbers. It made life easier, but got mucked about if the fleet was renumbered. Some did not care and took whatever was on offer, some being even more interesting in registering buses as they arrived like Bristol Omnibus Company's Lodekka FLF fleet, which had all sorts of registrations.

Some converted quite late, like Ribble which only started matching around 1963. So keen did it become that in 1967, when numbers were not available for new double-deckers as they had been taken for coaches, it numbered the new Leyland Atlantean double-deckers to match available registrations, 1951-65 if you are keen to know.

Registrations also illustrated the appalling delays in delivery of new buses endemic in the late 1960s and most of the 1970s. Operators booked registrations particularly to match fleetnumbers in time for the expected delivery which often turned out to be highly optimistic. In 1969, both Western Welsh and Cardiff took in buses with PKG plates. Western Welsh's 20 Leyland Leopards arrived in time to be PKG-G, but ten Atlanteans came after August so were PKG-H. Cardiff's 25 Daimler Fleetlines did not appear until October, hardly making it in time for the final trolleybus replacement for which some were destined and were firmly PKG-H

Then in the 1970s, like so much else it all went wrong. From about 1974 on there was a huge amalgamation of offices and registrations. Cardiff buses got county numbers, Newport Cardiff ones and Ribble Lancashire plates. I remember our relief there when the 1976 Atlantean AN68s arrived as NRN-P. 'Ah, proper Ribble registrations,' someone said.

Even an S breached Hadrian's Wall, WS going to Bristol and very odd it looked too. Additionally, for a while, authorities refused to allocate numbers on request, so matching with fleetnumbers went out the window. It all went horribly wrong and a new

start had to be made later in 1974 when, thankfully, nobody was using the start letter G, so most went back there and started over.

The end result of this was that registrations became far less part of the provenance of the bus and less of an interest for the enthusiast. The growth in the use of cherished plates did not help. The present system is so vague, making matching fleetnumbers no longer possible and many operators letting builders register buses, that it has become meaningless apart from giving a clue if an Alexander Dennis was built in Falkirk or Scarborough.

Registrations could cause amusement. Casual observers in Cardiff may well wonder what elbow and oboe Daimlers were. They were registered LBO and OBO. Red & White had two REs known as Gaxic and Gwoid. Well you can work that one out.

Stories abounded about buses coming out of overhaul with different plates on front and back. When Washington DC open-top operations were in the hands of MCW Metrobuses, I saw one that was Hull on the front and London on the back. On a visit to ECW at Lowestoft, the place was full of Bristol LHs destined for Hants & Dorset. I noticed the registrations were nothing to do with Bournemouth and pointed it out. 'Two letters sounded the same over the phone, we have to change them all,' was the reply.

Registrations lack such interest today and are a loss to our hobby.

A fleet list could not describe how a MCW Orion body could look pretty good on many buses, particularly those with an exposed radiator, but truly awful on tin front Leylands. Rhondda 418, with non-matching Glamorgan registration TTX 996, was a 1956 Weymann-built example on an AEC Regent V. It is in typical surroundings with a coal mine near Trehadog. This bus was new before the short-lived use of Scottish-style destination displays. ROY MARSHALL/THE BUS ARCHIVE

What did they look like?

Much of all this can be gleaned from fleet lists. But for some aspects, you had to be there. One of the most striking was how buses looked. Vehicles that sounded the same on paper could be radically different when you saw them in the metal.

Perhaps the most striking was the Metro-Cammell Weymann Orion body, a style that does divide opinion. But generally it was not a bad looking bus on AEC Regents, Daimlers, Guys and exposed radiator Leylands, But put it on a tin front Leyland of either type, and the result was truly atrocious. The front upper deck was pinched in, which in contrast to the fat lower deck front was dreadful. Goodness knows why. It was unnecessary, as some of Blackpool's later Titans proved.

Operators had their own tastes, Birmingham favoured postwar a rather gaunt Edwardian style produced by several builders to the same specification. Manchester had its Crossley-inspired drooping front windows and stepped waist rails, applied by other bodybuilders. Nottingham devised a style for rear-engined double-deckers which it standardised on for many years, probably too many, and it was supplied by various bodybuilders.

Park Royal devised a double-deck rear engine style for Sheffield which became known as that city style. Bodybuilders offered these styles to others, so generally were producing various styles at the same time. A Park Royal Atlantean for Sheffield and Fleetline for London looked totally different. So would Cardiff and Nottingham Willowbrook-bodied Fleetlines, Roe Fleetlines for Doncaster and Rotherham and Northern Counties-bodied Fleetlines for Yorkshire Traction and Teesside.

Some operators took other operators' styles. Edinburgh had Daimlers like Birmingham standards, Nottingham styles went to Burton and Tyne & Wear, and MCW built the distinctive Liverpool-style Atlantean, very different from others of that bodybuilder, for Bury and Bolton.

East Lancs went through a phase of building double-deckers almost identical to Alexander's. The iconic curved screen BET-style single deck could be bodied by any number of firms, as could the previous boxy style. None of this could be picked up on paper.

Coaches were a bit different as builders often gave them names, and it was usually the case that each type would look the same as that was part of the sales in a competitive market where looks mattered

A fleetlist would tell you that Edinburgh Corporation Alexander-bodied Leyland Titan 653 (ASC 653B) was a PD3/6, an exposed radiator type. That was how the chassis was delivered in 1964, but the operator standardised on a home-made glassfibre bonnet and grille of the previous Leyland type. You would only find that out by going there. Edinburgh also used big route and fleetnumbers. ROY MARSHALL/THE BUS ARCHIVE

The first Western Welsh buses with route number blinds came in 1958 with six of these Weymann-bodied Leyland Olympians, although the driver of this one had decided not to avail himself of it. Originally a dual purpose vehicle, Cardiff-registered 1488 had gained bus livery by June 1969 here in Caerphilly. The red is significantly lighter than that used by nearby fellow BET company Rhondda. ROY MARSHALL/THE BUS ARCHIVE

considerably. Today, if you read it on paper, you can almost guarantee that in the metal it will look exactly as you expect.

Destination displays

Destination displays varied considerably. The state-owned Tilling fleets with their standardised buses and liveries had broadly similar destination displays, so you could guess what you would see. BET was much more varied, often reflecting personal taste.

The state-owned Scottish Bus Group also had a standard display almost triangular from the mid-1950s and postwar, BET's Ribble adopted that idea too; maybe it was geographical proximity. But Rhondda used it briefly too and that was nowhere near Scotland. Western Welsh, despite showing route numbers in timetables, did not show them on buses until 1958 and then, unusually for the time, used yellow on black for numbers.

Derby 114, a Northern Counties-bodied Volvo Ailsa, in the city centre during September 1982 may have been running along Coleridge Street rather than terminating there. A good idea was putting a number 1 in front of the route number to denote driver-only operation. ROY MARSHALL/THE BUS ARCHIVE

Nottingham managed a revision to its previously mainly green livery that suited both rear- and front-engined double-deckers, something not all achieved. Park Royal-bodied AEC Regent V 225 demonstrates this in October 1972. This was another operator to use the term City and big route numbers. GEOFFREY MORANT

It was in the municipal field where you knew least what to expect and it often reflected personal taste. A change could often signal the arrival of a new general manager. Big numbers as in Belfast and Manchester seemed a good idea to me as this was the best indication of exactly where the bus was going. This process was highlighted in Cardiff, where having achieved almost the ideal with its 1972 Fleetlines, it reverted to tiny numbers and small screens on the 1974 Bristol VRTs.

The destination itself was fascinating, giving all sorts of ideas about places served and they were often an excuse for a picture. Hotwells in Bristol, Dangerous Corner in Wigan and Electric House in Ipswich all seemed to suggest peril, and some of my fellow students took some years to find out that a Sheffield 95 to Intake was actually going to a place not a description like Private.

Circulars posed a problem, merely saying circular gave no idea of direction, so some clue was necessary. Newport and Birmingham solved it by using A or C to show direction (anticlockwise or clockwise). Derby and Hull were unusual in often using the American system of showing the main road served. In one case, owing to a one way system, the buses no longer served the road on the blind.

Many operators had distinctive destination lettering styles, Sheffield a great example. But the move to lower case lettering in my view was a legibility disaster. Ribble's Oswaltwhistle Town End became a white stripe. Route identification varied too, most using numbers, but some like Exeter, Preston and Oldham used letters. Big operators often had to use letter prefixes as there were not enough numbers around, but Crosville used it as standard, as did Midland General

Electronics, while more versatile, have taken a long time to become as clear as roller blinds but are getting there. But, owing to their nature, it is sometimes difficult to capture a destination in a picture, so another loss to our hobby.

Livery applications

Fleet lists gave fleetnumbers, but how were they applied? Hardly anyone used the same styles and locations. Some, including a few Tilling operators like Crosville and United Counties had fleetnumber plates, the Scottish Bus Group all sorts, which gave added interest. Reading sported big transfers, Southdown small and East Kent none at all, relying on registrations. Manchester and Leeds had little ones on the front, big ones on the back. A few fleets like Neath & Cardiff did not show them externally at all.

And so to liveries, always certain to cause debate and very much a matter of taste, particularly of those who decide. Here paper descriptions were pretty hopeless.

You really could not rely on fleet lists to give you any idea what Walsall's buses would look like. You had to go there. No.401 was a lightweight Daimler CVG5 with a body built by the operator on Metal Sections frames. It took a while to finish the job, as 401 entered service in 1956 two years after two fellow chassis bodied by Northern Counties. This also shows the odd front windscreens specified by Walsall on its Daimler Fleetlines. Another operator with big route and fleet numbers and a striking livery.
ROY MARSHALL/THE BUS ARCHIVE

All major company operators in south Wales were red, but the three BETs, Rhondda, Western Welsh and South Wales all used different shades, with the Tilling companies United Welsh and Red & White using a fourth shade, standard corporate red. Cardiff, West Mon and Merthyr all had colours that could be described as maroon, but all were different.

Bradford and East Yorkshire buses were both blue and cream on paper but could not be more different. Dundee, Aberdeen, Lincoln, Southdown and Maidstone & District were all green and cream, but bore little resemblance. Nothing on paper could prepare you for Halifax, Glasgow, Sheffield and Accrington. You had to be there.

Some fleets updated their liveries, keeping the same colours with varying degrees of success. Nottingham managed it with a scheme that worked on both front- and rear-engined types. Newport was more radical, copying Dinky Toys, but it worked surprisingly well. Less so were the inexplicable pale blue and white so-called lowheight livery in West Bromwich, wishy washy green and white in Bury and Walsall's insipid pale blue and white on its immense 36ft Fleetline No.56 of 1968. Yorkshire Traction went from staid to racy simply by changing lettering and numbering styles.

Individual liveries not only gave individuality but could brighten a place up. Walsall's powder blue, Bradford's cheery blue, Newcastle's yellow, to say

nothing of Sheffield, Halifax and Glasgow were exceptional at this, but smart red Huddersfield managed it too.

There was a sudden blue phase which overtook Derby, Brighton, Preston and West Mon. It was a dramatic change and all looked pretty good but did they all fit?

The advent of PTEs swept much of this away replacing them with what I consider to be bland corporateness. None of their liveries suited front-engined buses, although things were not too bad in the early days of Merseyside and Tyneside. Selnec chose orange not because of what it was, but what it was not, like nothing before. It started a mini orange tide sweeping over Cardiff, Merthyr and Grimsby-Cleethorpes. Then came National Bus Company corporate identity. Like them or not, they swept away a huge part of our interest .

Deregulation brought a welcome splash of colour rather swiftly snuffed out by the big groups' corporate hues. Of late, this stranglehold has been loosened and with modern day technology, more striking liveries have appeared, giving a reason to travel for a look. Sadly, the spectre of franchising threatens the return of dull bland utilitarian images giving no encouragement to lure the customer on board. Nor enthusiasts to visit? ∎

· *Images enhanced by MICHAEL EYRE*

Devoted to Daimlers

In words and pictures, **LAURENCE KNIGHT** shares his passion for the Daimler halfcabs that were a feature of the quiet East Midlands town of Northampton for 50 years and which it bought from the late 1930s to the late 1960s

From an early age, rides on a red Northampton Corporation bus meant travelling on a Daimler CVG6. Unsurprising, since from 1964 to 1972 this was the only type it operated. Yet variety existed among this standardisation, and even as a four-year-old I had my favourites.

Imagine my mother's embarrassment at my bus stop tantrums if a newer one hove into view; earlier Daimlers were fitted with gloriously melodious gearboxes, of great appeal to my five-year-old ears. On one school day, the conductor had to haul me away from her and on to the platform of a non-musical 1960s model. Some mothers do 'ave 'em...

Conductors and drivers often were permanent pairings. It was always a joy to be travelling on an older Daimler, but my face would positively light up on seeing a certain clippie, knowing that her driver would always use first gear, treating his audience to the full repertoire of Daimler orchestrations. All complemented by lashings of varnished wood and leather, lending a Dickensian air to proceedings.

One of the few redeeming aspects of attending the cold and draughty St James' Voluntary Primary School (not that my attendance was voluntary) was the ride home. The school special was often one of my favoured early CVG6s, whose chilly, smoky interior spoke of a lack of activity before the school run. More frightening than any teacher, however, were the formidable clippies who would dispense clips of the ear at the least provocation.

Last and first: Northampton 267 (JVV 267G), the last Roe-bodied Daimler CVG6 for the municipal fleet and the last 27ft CVG6 built for anybody, has been retained in preservation, now in the care of Northampton Transport Heritage. It was new in 1968. These later vehicles had the wider front axle and cowl, more common on 30ft Daimlers. The inset, from the author's picture collection, shows 103 (VV 7875) from the 1939 delivery of Roe-bodied Daimler COG5s.

Preserved 1945 Daimler CWD6 129 (VV 8934), a Duple-bodied utility with a Daimler CD6 engine, at a running day in Lincoln in 2018. ADRIAN PEARSON

Creature comforts such as heaters were incorporated in later buses, and the dim, twinkling tungsten bulbs – bane of elderly conductors struggling to complete their waybills at night – ceded to brighter, clinical fluorescent tubes.

By 1970, all of the earlier models had gone, leaving Northampton with 68 near-identical Roe-bodied CVG6s. Archaic maybe, but certainly not ancient. Some were barely two years old. Finally, in 1972, it was dragged kicking and screaming into line with the rest of the world, and introduced one-person operation with 20 Fleetline single-deckers with Leyland engines and Willowbrook bodies. They were Daimlers too, but not CVG6s.

Preselector predecessors

The story of Northampton's Daimlers starts in the 1930s. The boffins at Daimler stumbled upon what was to become the Holy Grail of bus transmission, by combining a preselector gearbox – where the desired ratio was chosen in advance by positioning a lever, then selected by pressing a pedal – with a fluid coupling, producing a bus which took the hard work out of gear changing.

Smooth acceleration from a standstill was guaranteed — the fluid flywheel replaced the clutch — and it was impossible not to engage the desired gear. With just a little care and attention,

silky smooth gearchanges could be executed, and driving in heavy traffic became a doddle. No more juddering clutch, no careful matching of revs, no more grating and grinding. Even hands-free changes on roundabouts were possible.

AEC, builder of London's buses, saw the advantages and pending the development of its own Wilson gearbox (as it was named, after its inventor), bought Daimler 'boxes for London's STL-class Regents.

Roe-bodied Crossley DD42/3 143 (VV 9143), one of Northampton's first ten postwar buses, operating hilly and busy route 25 in 1960. Because of their crash gearboxes, these became restricted to lighter duties as newer Daimlers were delivered. BRIAN HOLLOWAY

Northampton was at the front of the queue for the new Daimler CVG6 in 1947, receiving 20 with Northern Coachbuilders bodies, several of which reached their 20th birthday. This shows the doyen of the batch, 150 (ANH 150), in Abington Street. AUTHOR'S COLLECTION

Just as astute as the preselector was its marriage to the Gardner engine. Prewar bus bodies were lighter, so the highly reliable and economical 5LW was the usual choice. A ride on a Bristol K5G, with the same engine bolted to the chassis, ferociously assaulted eardrums and rattled fillings, but thanks

to sound deadening, a prewar Daimler was quieter than a 1970s Fleetline.

And so the COG5 was born, a vehicle that was easy to drive and pleasant to ride in. The Daimler gearbox produced a beautiful, melodious sound, at its sweetest in first gear, the perfect accompaniment to travel. AEC's version of the gearbox created its own delicious melody; an RT accelerating away in second gear was as iconic as the chimes of Big Ben. Guy also offered a preselector gearbox after the war; Guys were not known for their reticence, and competing with their rasping exhausts was a particularly soulful gearbox song, featuring a distinctive second gear growl and, of course, the trademark Guy whistle.

Competition time

By the 1930s, Northampton was losing interest in running trams, and if they were to be replaced by motorbuses, an easy-change gearbox would greatly assist the tram men in their transition. After the departure of the last trams in 1934, general manager John Cameron ordered two demonstrators that fitted the bill, all-Leyland 'Gearless' Titan

Eighteen years' evolution of Roe-bodied CVG6s are in this view in Mercers Row. Exposed radiator 188 (ANH 188) of 1950 lasted for nearly 20 years, but 260 (GNH 260F) from the 1967 delivery only managed 13, a victim of the rush to convert to one-person operation. These were tough times for the corporation in 1968, but the advertisements on the front raised some revenue, and the shallower destination displays (masked down on 188) economised on blind length. ROY MARSHALL/THE BUS ARCHIVE

Northampton's first 8ft wide bus, 190 (DNH 190), was retained to enable trainees to have a broader driving experience than that of tuition bus 154. It survived in this guise until 1978, when extensive corrosion sealed its fate. All 8ft wide CVG6s apart from the final batch had narrow-tracked front axles, with the Roe body gently tapered in at the front to match. This shows 190 entering Greyfriars Bus Station in September 1976, with 210 (JVV 210) of 1959 behind. ALAN MILLAR

TD4c 83 (BTB 613) and Strachans-bodied Daimler COG5 84 (BVC 268).

The Leyland was years ahead of its time, employing a torque convertor which eased the bus to around 20mph. A lever was then activated to engage solid drive. Today's Voith gearboxes operate in a similar fashion, albeit with more gears and automatic control.

The Daimler was the more successful design. The Leyland probably spent most of its time in torque convertor mode, making it sluggish and thirsty. The legendary economy of the Daimler's Gardner engine yielded an impressive 11mpg.

The decision to go with Gardner-engined preselector Daimlers cast the die for the next 30-plus years' vehicle purchases and thus was born a vision in vermillion that was as pleasing to the eye as the ear. The metallic clatter of the Gardner engine was subdued by Daimler's sound insulation; the quiet, refined personality of the later 1960s models was just what would be expected from the manufacturer of cars for royalty, though with the result that some dismissed them as boring.

Sixteen COG5s with English Electric bodies were followed by Northampton's dream combination in 1939, Daimlers with solid, teak-framed Roe bodies. Numbers 101-10 (VV 7873-7, 8202-6), known by local enthusiasts as the 'One-ohs', withstood the heavy loadings and postponed maintenance of the war and survived for over 20 years.

Northampton is traditionally associated with shoemaking, and during the war years was tasked with keeping the forces well shod. Thus the transport department was allocated 27 utility versions of its favoured marque. These were mainly Duple- and Roe-bodied; AEC and Daimler engines were also thrown into the mix. Hopes were pinned, however, on an eventual return to the Daimler/Gardner/Roe combination.

Beggars cannot be choosers

The constraints of the war years took time to ease, so operators made do with whatever was available. Luckily, in 1946 the Roe factory in Leeds supplied ten bodies to postwar specification, vehicles that proved to be very sturdy.

By contrast, even the early postwar bodies of highly-respected Eastern Coach Works — obliged, like many, to make do with unseasoned timber — suffered from pillar rot. Daimler could not provide quick delivery, so Crossleys featured in this first peacetime-standard delivery, and armchair driving had to take a back seat, as constant mesh (crash) gearboxes returned to the fleet.

Some operators found the DD42/3 model to be underpowered, and the added challenge of the gearboxes caused Northampton to restrict these buses, 140-9, mainly to the flatter east-west routes. Characterful and with enormous enthusiast appeal, the Crossleys were less well thought of by

Five of the ten 1953 CVG6s had Roe bodies built on Park Royal frames. Their distinctive styling had echoes of the London RT, perpetuated by the newly-adopted livery of red with a single narrow band. This is 197 (DNH 197) passing the Manfield shoe factory. It is now in preservation. JOHN EVANS

the engineers, and only served to reinforce the superiority of the Daimler.

My only recollection of a ride on a Crossley in service is of a droning back axle, underlining the spares problem of later years. Enthusiastic drivers may have enjoyed the challenge of their gearboxes, but for most, the sneaky positioning of a Crossley outside the garage door was enough to dissuade them from running in to the depot for a bus change.

V for victory

Things moved on apace in 1947. For many Daimler operators, Gardner engines were preferred, and to match the heavier bodywork associated with postwar deliveries, the six-cylinder 6LW became standard. And so the CVG6 was born – the V standing for victory. Daimler would have preferred its own CD6-engined variant (CVD6) to become its standard — which it was in single-deck form — but it bowed to customer pressure and Gardners won the day.

Coventry City Transport had a predilection for AECs, squaring its dilemma over whether to buy local products by opting for Daimlers with AEC's 7.7litre engine (CVA6), and a small minority, such as Manchester, stuck with the 5LW in CVG5s.

For Northampton, the CVG6 represented perfection, and its long love affair with the type produced, in later years, the curious situation where CVG6s replaced CVG6s. The first arrivals were among the first deliveries anywhere in the country; a record-breaking (for Northampton) 20, numbered 150-69 (ANH 150-69), arrived in 1947; 153 was the first of its type supplied to a British operator.

The impact of the new buses on the war-torn fleet was immense. Distinctive Northern Coachbuilders bodies were accepted for quick delivery, featuring large, owlish front upper deck windows, and the same bell-shaped rear upper deck emergency exits that had been adopted for London trolleybuses. However, before long an ominous body sag (thanks to the use of unseasoned timber framing) afflicted many, including Northampton's.

The appearance of these early CVG6s was affected by the length of the Gardner 6LW engine, which caused the radiator to protrude, and the hindquarters to be trimmed, to keep the bus within length limits. This impressionable five-year-old was

Later CVG6s received Roe four-bay bodies of this general appearance, but 200-9 of 1957 had Birmingham-style fronts which, combined with larger destination screens, gave them a dignified, haughty appearance. Those screens, intended for the larger displays of earlier blinds, were masked down from new, as eventually were those of many older buses.
AUTHOR'S COLLECTION

struck by their porcine profile and bouncy backend, referring to the Northern Coachbuilders-bodied Daimlers as 'piggy buses'. My mother really must have wondered what was in my orange Smarties.

Those 20 Daimlers benefited from Northampton's good maintenance and lasted a creditable 17 to 19 years. Solid Roe bodies returned on later Daimlers and were probably capable of even greater longevity, but the onset of one-person operation, and generous bus grants, meant the potential of late models was rarely achieved.

The first Roe-bodied CVG6s came in 1949/50 in two almost identical batches of ten — 170-89 (ANH 170-89). Richly-varnished woodwork, handsome bodies that sat proud and erect on their chassis, mellifluously ululating transmissions…an engaging ensemble that made for buses with great passenger appeal, and a lifespan not achieved by subsequent batches.

Honed by evolution

Evolution took place through subsequent deliveries as Roe gradually honed its standard product. The demise of Northern Coachbuilders caused 1953 buses 190-9, earmarked for its products, also to receive Roe bodies; 195-9 were built on Park Royal frames, complemented by a new, rationalised livery of red with one central band; maybe some London Transport influence here. Four-bay bodies, a raked front and vertical rear, they were almost a Daimler version of the RT.

NCT quietly and pragmatically pursued a regular fleet renewal programme of ten, then six new

CVG6s in most years. Only small modifications, if any, existed between many batches, as the innovation of the 1930s declined into stolid conservatism.

The 1953 buses were the last with by then outdated exposed radiators. Fluorescent interior lighting had to wait until the 1964 delivery, and the Daimatic semi-automatic gearbox, adopted by many, was eschewed, as was the rear-engined Fleetline. The final 1968 examples, 263-7 (JVV 263-7G), stubbornly remained 59-seat, 27ft buses with open rear platforms. Northampton's buying policy was out of step, and the fuel economy of its CVG6s was negated by their modest capacity and two-person crews.

A slowdown in the purchase of new buses took place through the 1950s and 1960s. A drop in passenger numbers, caused by increased car ownership and the decline of cinemas and theatres, followed by labour shortages and strikes in the late 1960s, gradually reduced mileage and fleet strength.

Ninety-one buses dwindled to 68. It was sad to peer into St James' depot in 1969 to see the serried ranks of 15 withdrawn buses, and even sadder to see how empty the depot seemed after they had gone. Much loved though the 1950 Daimlers were, their time was up; this could not be said of the 1953 batch, many of which had only recently been overhauled, including a typically high-quality repaint and varnish.

Fleetline faux-pas

Inertia set in. The transport department plodded on for three years with its 68 near-identical CVG6s, while contemplating its future choice of vehicle.

Before the opening of Greyfriars Bus Station in May 1976, corporation services departed from town centre streets, although in bad weather it was possible to wait in the comfort of an open platform Daimler. But this was a warm, sunny day in the Drapery, with 237 (RNH 237) and 236 (RNH 236) of 1963. The emergency exit could be propped open for ventilation. Was this a unique Northampton feature?

In Mercers Row on a wet Sunday in August 1973 is 257 (ENH 257D) from the 1966 delivery, with a single-deck Fleetline parked in the background. ALAN MILLAR

The local newspaper, the *Chronicle & Echo,* allowed its journalists free rein, suggesting something from the space age...a high capacity double-decker bristling with contemporary gimmicks and gizmos, such as closed-circuit television cameras and sensors to detect seat occupancy.

Reality proved different. It was not aliens that scared the pigeons off the roof of All Saints' Church in the town centre but the raucous roar of a Leyland 680 engine mounted in a Willowbrook-bodied 45-seat single-deck Fleetline, struggling away in second gear in the officially-approved NCT manner.

The Fleetline was a great success as a double-decker, emulating and improving on the early Leyland Atlantean by offering a drop-centre rear axle which permitted lowheight bodywork, and the economical Gardner engine. Neither benefit was accorded to Fleetlines 1-20 (UNH 1-20L), which were delivered in 1972, though not unleashed on the general public en masse until April 1973, owing to union resistance to one-person operation.

The weight and vibration of a heavy engine perched at the end of an extended 36ft chassis did not take long to create major stress, both to the bodywork and to Northampton's engineers. Rear windows moved independently of bodywork

before threatening to fall out completely. Bodywork integrity was compromised by centre doors, which also caused the tragic death of an elderly woman who, while exiting the bus, became trapped between bus and railings which had been intended to protect passengers queuing for rear-loaders.

The double-deck Fleetline was not without its faults, but a Roe-bodied CRG6LXB, with the benefit of good maintenance, undemanding schedules and generally sympathetic driving, would have been ideal for Northampton.

The failings of the single-deckers led to their early demise. Bus 1 was appropriately the first; by 1981 it was dumped behind the depot minus engine, rear window and much else, resembling a greenhouse without glass. Meanwhile, CVG6s plodded on, but with widespread one-person operation became restricted to fewer areas of the town.

The next best thing?

Northampton Borough Transport, as it became after the local government reorganisation of 1974, had a brief flirtation with Leyland Nationals, before reverting to double-deckers with 36 Alexander-bodied Bristol VRTs from 1977 onwards. Fortunately, Northampton was expanding with

London overspill estates to the east of the town, spawning a burgeoning and lucrative network of one-person operated routes.

Not everyone was a fan of Northampton's VRTs. The hiccups and jerks of its over-enthusiastic automatic gear control, combined with lightweight highbridge bodywork, made for a bouncy, uncomfortable ride. This contrasted dramatically with the stately, unflappable CVG6s, creeping gently away in second gear, saving fuel...London Transport influence once again, maybe.

Northampton was no slouch when it came to fiscal rectitude. Worn seat cushions and other components were retained, to be swapped for those of withdrawn stock, and a CVG6 with limited life expectancy might yield its good gearbox for a worn-out one. But it was the VRs — reliable workhorses and using even less fuel than a CVG6 — that really benefited the finances.

The rapid conversion of most services to one-person operation compensated for the lack of innovation of earlier years. But the reversing procedure required at the terminus of the 13 at Links View Estate caused the retention of three

Daimlers, 261/6/7 (GNH 261F, JVV 266/7G). The reversing problem became history, along with scheduled CVG6 operation, with the construction of a turning circle in 1985. The last two Fleetlines, 6 and 7, lingered on until 1986, ending the Daimler love affair.

Well, almost. No.267 was retained on account of its historic interest – the last open-platform, preselector, teak-framed bus — along with former training bus 154 from the original 1947 batch. In 1993, the by now arm's-length Northampton Transport company was sold to GRT Bus Group, which became part of FirstBus in 1995 and both 154 and 267 passed initially to the 154 Preservation Group.

These survivors are now in the safe hands of Northampton Transport Heritage, which as a registered charity maintains a prominent profile in the town, doing an excellent job of bringing the past alive. During the year there are several opportunities to roll back the years, with 146, 154 and 267 among others kept active on civic events, rallies and running days, and — as part of the trust's educational role — visits to schools in the area... without the acerbic clippie. ■

Daimlers served Northampton for over 35 years, ending on May 2, 1986 when Willowbrook-bodied Fleetline SRL6-36 No.6 (UNH 6L) operated the last scheduled Daimler journey for Northampton Transport, the honour of driving it falling to management trainee David Pike, who prepared a small commemorative sign. By then, 16 of the 20 had already been scrapped, but this one was painted in Northampton Borough Council yellow and black, ready for conversion into an exhibition unit. The small green sign is an understated expression of discomfort over the forthcoming deregulation of bus services.

Change of
ownership

Thirty years after they were privatised, London's big red bus companies are all in foreign ownership. **ALAN MILLAR** looks at how that happened, when and why

U
ntil 1994, most of London Transport's red buses were state-owned. In one of the major acts of privatisation, its ten operating companies were sold to new private sector owners, all of which were British. Thirty years on, not only are they all owned by businesses ultimately based abroad, but three-and-a-bit of the ten companies of 1994 are subsidiaries of companies owned by European states.

This is not the place to judge whether that is right or wrong. It has happened. But it may be enlightening to consider how and why it happened.

London was left out when the rest of Britain's buses — in Scotland, Wales and 'provincial' England — were deregulated in October 1986 and the state-owned National Bus Company (NBC) and Scottish Bus Group (SBG) were privatised respectively in 1986-88 and 1990/91. It escaped or missed out — delete whichever suits your point of view — because the same Conservative government that pursued deregulation had put London's transport through its own regulatory change two years earlier.

London Transport had been taken out of the control of the Greater London Council in 1984 and into a new state-owned organisation, London Regional Transport that minimised the use of Regional in its day-to-day self-description. Its bus and Underground operations were put into new subsidiary companies, with London Buses

Each of the new London Buses subsidiary companies had the same style of fleetname accompanied by a logo, which in the case of London General was a pre-World War One B Type double-decker. This is VC1, a Northern Counties-bodied Volvo Citybus with registration 101 CLT originally on Routemaster RM1101. MIKE HARRIS

Metroline added a blue skirt to its livery post-privatisation, as on East Lancs Olympus-bodied Scania N230UD SEL763 (LK07 BDE). By the time it was delivered the company was owned by ComfortDelGro whose name accompanies Metroline's on the fleetname. MARK LYONS

required to bid competitively with other operators as its routes were put out to tender. The difference with the rest of the country was that competition occurred before rather than after buses went on the streets.

Periodically, transport ministers said this was a passing phase; that London's buses would eventually be deregulated, but the tendering phase never passed.

Smaller units

In preparation for the day that it might happen, and for when the capital's state-owned buses were privatised, London Buses was divided into smaller businesses that would be more digestible by private sector buyers and also be focused on their local markets and ready to compete in a deregulated environment.

In April 1989, the main operations were split into 11 companies. Clockwise from south of the River Thames, these were Selkent (short for South East London & Kent), London Central, South London, London General, London United, CentreWest, Metroline, London Northern, Leaside, London Forest and East London.

Those with a knowledge of transport history would recognise London Central, London General and London United as names of former bus or tram operators and those attuned to more recent times knew that Selkent, Forest and Leaside were names London Transport had given to three of the districts created in an earlier devolution of management.

Much more important than the names were the people in charge. Some were from within the organisation, mainly rising stars among past intakes of graduate management trainees, while others had worked for NBC or municipal operators, bringing not only an understanding of how things could be done differently but also of the cut and thrust of deregulation.

Along with these 11 companies were two others. One was Stanwell Buses, which called itself Westlink and operated in some of the same south-western suburbs as London United. It had been set up in August 1986 as a low-cost operation run along the lines of the independent businesses that had been winning tendered service contracts.

The other was London Coaches, created in January 1986 to operate the Round London Sightseeing Tour and other commercial activities

London United's privatisation livery, with grey skirt and white roof, was revived in 2014 as a heritage livery on Scania OmniCity SP40102. By then, the company was part of the RATP Group. MARK BAILEY

that included, for a time, express coach services linking London with Birmingham and Eastbourne. It later became a significant operator of commuter coach services into London from Kent.

The privatisation of NBC was drawn out from the period immediately before deregulation in October 1986 to March 1988. The first companies to be sold were better placed to focus on the challenges of on-the-road competition than those going through the protracted sale process, so alarm bells rang when the government indicated in 1991 that its instinct for London was to deregulate first. It was persuaded to take the opposite course and had effectively given up on deregulation when Labour came to power in 1997.

Selling the London companies became a priority, but there was one fewer than in 1989. London Forest was closed in 1991, with most of its work either lost or divided between Leaside and East London. A year earlier, Bexleyheath garage was transferred from Selkent to London Central following a tendered service win.

Westlink and London Coaches had to be sold to clear the decks for the big show when bids would be invited for the main operations. The sightseeing operator Guide Friday was selected early in 1992 as preferred bidder for London Coaches, but pulled out for a variety of reasons that included the economics of using open-top Routemasters rather than its preferred choice of rear-engined

double-deckers: too few top deck seats to sell, too many staff to crew them. A management buyout, named Pullman Group, bought it later that year.

Westlink was sold to its management in January 1994. Go-Ahead Group — of which more shortly — was preferred bidder but pulled out. The buyout lasted three months, as West Midlands Travel bought 90% of the equity as a stepping stone towards what it hoped might be a bigger presence in London.

The big sale

The ten main companies were offered for sale in March 1994. Management-led teams would be allowed a 5% preference over outside bidders in the price paid and no bidder could buy more than two companies.

This all happened against rapid change in the landscape of the bus industry. Many of the management buyouts from NBC had either sold out to emerging new groups or turned themselves into groups. The bargain prices paid for many NBC companies — National Express was the only one to reach (just) double figures of millions and most went for less than £5million — were unlikely to be repeated in the London sale.

Four of the new groups — Badgerline, Go-Ahead, GRT, National Express and Stagecoach — were floated on the London stock exchange between December 1992 and April 1994 to raise funds for future expansion. Another potential buyer, Cowie group, was already a listed PLC.

First to be sold, in September 1994, was CentreWest. Its management team raised £25.6million for what would be the first of four management buyouts. The others were at London General, London United and Metroline.

CentreWest's managing director, Peter Hendy, then 41, was one of London Transport's rising stars, a product of the graduate development scheme whose star would rise farther than others', ultimately to the House of Lords as a crossbench peer on a route that took him to FirstGroup, MD of surface transport and subsequently commissioner (chief executive by another name) at Transport for London, then chair of Network Rail, and honours as a CBE and knight.

Two of the newly floated PLCs also triumphed. Stagecoach bought East London and Selkent, while Go-Ahead netted London Central. Stagecoach had begun life in Scotland 14 years earlier as a long distance express operator with a handful of coaches, bought three companies from NBC in 1987, two more in the SBG privatisation and mopped up several of the NBC management buyouts. Go-Ahead grew out of the 1987 management buyout of NBC's Northern General and began acquiring other NBC buyouts in southern England.

Cowie also triumphed by acquiring Leaside and South London, the latter company not being sold until January 1995 as it had run into trouble over maintenance standards; Cowie was persuaded to buy it, flattered by compliments about the high standard of engineering at Leaside.

Its success was a turning point for a business that until then regarded buses as a sideline. It was based in Sunderland and since 1938 had grown from a motorcycle retailer into one of the country's biggest car and van dealers and leasing companies. Its bus industry involvement began by accident in 1980 when it acquired the George Ewer Group, primarily for its dealerships.

Ewer also owned Grey-Green Coaches in London and rather than sell that part of the business, it restructured it, taking advantage of London Transport route tendering to turn it increasingly into a bus operator. The London Buses privatisation gave it a chance to grow much bigger in passenger transport. So much so that it acquired the non-listed British Bus group in 1996, renamed itself Arriva in late 1997 and soon pulled out of car and van sales to focus on buses and trains in the UK and mainland Europe.

The other successful bidder was MTL, the employee buyout that had acquired Merseyside Transport Ltd, the arm's length bus operation of Merseyside PTE, in 1992. It took ownership of London Northern.

First's London livery in 2009, with yellow and white versions of the magenta and blue willow leaf stripes in its national livery, on VNE32052 (X578 RJW), the only East Lancs Vyking-bodied Volvo B7TL in the fleet. This bus was converted later into an engineering training classroom. MARK LYONS

Before the all-red rule was applied, Stagecoach adopted this London version of its national livery, with blue and orange swoops and a dark blue skirt. MARK LYONS

Badgerline and GRT, which both missed out at a time they were both making other significant acquisitions, merged in 1995 to create what then was FirstBus but later became FirstGroup as it added trains to its portfolio. Along with National Express, it would have its day in the London sun.

Quick onward sales

Nothing is guaranteed to last forever, least of all management buyouts backed by venture capitalists. At very least, they must expand and realistically they need to find a longer term owner. All four of the London buyouts were in new ownership within four years.

Go-Ahead acquired London General in May 1996 and combined the management teams. Within ten years, Keith Ludeman, the ex-Burnley & Pendle municipal MD who had headed London General since 1989, was the group's chief executive. Go-Ahead went on to acquire Metrobus in 1999, further strengthening its position in London.

CentreWest expanded in March 1996 to buy the remaining operations of Q Drive, one of the smaller outside buyers of ex-NBC companies. Q Drive had already sold most of the two former Alder Valley companies, but still had Beeline operations in parts of Berkshire as well as London Buslines, operating tendered services for London Transport.

CentreWest also broke out of its territory to win tendered contracts in Orpington, south-east London and could have grown even bigger as Stagecoach was

unhappy with the performance of Selkent and, never one to shirk a difficult decision, agreed a price to sell it to CentreWest in 1996, but the potential buyer's backers declined to raise the funds.

FirstGroup acquired CentreWest in March 1997, put Peter Hendy in charge of its bus operations across a large chunk of east and south-east England and acquired Capital Citybus from its management (led by future Transport for London surface transport MD Leon Daniels) in July 1998.

London United acquired Westlink from West Midlands Travel in January 1995 and in August 1997 became the first of the companies to pass into foreign hands when the French group Transdev, barely known in Britain before then, acquired it.

Metroline held out the longest. It placed shares on the stock market and made moves to expand, losing out to First when it bid for CentreWest but acquiring London Northern from MTL in August 1998, around the same time as it expanded 400miles away to purchase Scottish Citylink Coaches from National Express. However, its independence ended in March 2000 when sold to another foreign buyer, Singapore-based DelGro Corporation, which became ComfortDelGro in 2002. The group also owns SBS Transit, the principal bus operator in Singapore.

One early consequence of privatisation was a controlled relaxation of London bus liveries. While tendering from 1985 had brought a multiplicity of colours as new operators won contracts, the new owners of the privatised companies were required keep their buses red, but up to 20% of the body area could be given a unique look.

This was executed most noticeably by Metroline, which added a blue skirt (with particularly unobtrusive sensitivity on Routemasters) and by London United, with white roofs and top deck window surrounds on its rear-engined double-deckers.

Cowie applied yellow flashes, while as Arriva it had a London version of the Cotswold stone 'cow horns' that were a feature of its aquamarine livery elsewhere. Most of the others did subtle things with yellow, grey or white lining, though Stagecoach went for plain red but added orange and blue rear side swoops from its new national livery adopted towards the end of 2000.

MTL's approach at London Northern was less appealing, dropping a relief band and relying only on its large fleetname and logo to break up the red.

Operators' scope for such self-expression was limited after Transport for London was formed in July 2000, with standards tightened incrementally to reach the present position where red is the only the body colour, the transport authority's roundel is the main logo and the operator's fleetname is white and to an agreed (relatively small) size.

East Thames Buses

Something quite unexpected happened in early 2000, a few months before Transport for London replaced London Regional Transport and political accountability moved from central government to the new London Assembly: London Buses began operating buses again, albeit on a small scale.

One of the tendered service providers, Harris Bus of Grays, went into administration. No one rushed to buy the business and with drivers leaving for more secure employment elsewhere, London Buses took over and rebranded the organisation as East Thames Buses, with London red replacing Harris's blue and green.

It became an operator of last resort, taking on two additional routes south of the Thames after London Easylink collapsed in August 2002. It neither bid for tendered services nor was awarded contracts to run them, but was allocated work. It was sold to Go-Ahead in October 2009, finally ending British public ownership of London's buses.

This fitted into a wider picture of consolidation, with the privatised red bus companies acquiring smaller contractors.

Arriva integrated Grey-Green and the London operations of privatised ex-NBC companies into what had become its London North and London

East Thames Buses VP2 (X151 FBB), a Volvo B7TL with Plaxton President body. The bus and route 185 were taken over from London Easylink after that operator closed. MARK LYONS

The RATP Dev London Transit fleetname is below the driver's cab on OME46006 (YJ70 EVH), an electric Optare Metrodecker new to Tower Transit. ALAN MILLAR

South companies and bought the Original London Sightseeing Tour from London Coaches in December 1997. London Coaches closed in 2003.

Go-Ahead acquired Docklands Buses in September 2006, Blue Triangle in June 2007 and First's isolated CentreWest offshoot at Orpington in December 2007. Metroline bought the Armchair Passenger Transport and Thorpe's businesses in 2004. Stagecoach purchased Docklands Transit in July 1997 along with Transit Holdings' other operations in Devon and Oxford. Transdev bought London Sovereign from Blazefield Holdings in November 2002 and NSL Services seven years later.

Other ownership changes were a result of strategic decisions by the larger operators. The first was in June 2006, when Stagecoach sold its London business to the Australian-owned Macquarie Bank, which renamed it East London Bus Group. Macquarie paid £264million for it but sold it back to Stagecoach in October 2010 for just £59.4million.

First retreats

First's disposal of the Orpington offshoot was a foretaste of what followed after founding chief executive Sir Moir Lockhead retired in 2011 and the group began to sell or close underperforming businesses. Among these was its entire London operation, which was taking up a disproportionate share of capital investment, causing it to offload mid-life London buses into regional fleets that wanted more say over what they bought.

Go-Ahead bought the Northumberland Park garage of what had been First Capital in March 2012, while in June 2013 Metroline bought five former CentreWest garages, and Tower Transit, a new venture by Australian operator Transit Systems, bought the other two CentreWest garages and the former First Capital garage at Lea Interchange. Go-Ahead took over First's remaining contracts in the eastern suburbs.

Things also were becoming complicated in France. Transdev merged in 2010 with Veolia Transport, another French multinational, to form Veolia Transdev, but state-owned RATP Dev, the commercial arm of the Paris bus and metro operator, owned a stake in Transdev. To disentangle that, some Veolia Transdev businesses were transferred to RATP and London United became an RATP subsidiary in March 2011. Transdev retained London Sovereign for another three years, before selling it to RATP, which also acquired the Original London Sightseeing Tour from Arriva in 2014.

Into the midst of all this came two other significant players. One was National Express. It had acquired West Midlands Travel in April 1995 and the following year rebranded it as Travel West Midlands which, in turn, won contracts to operate two tendered London routes from June 1998, trading as Travel London. It sold that venture to another contractor, Limebourne, in August 2000.

Limebourne was sold to French-owned Connex Bus a year later, but National Express bought the Connex venture in February 2004, reviving the Travel London name. It expanded in June 2005 to take over the London and Surrey buses of Tellings-Golden Miller. But the group's involvement in London ended again in May 2009 with the sale of Travel London to Abellio, a subsidiary of the Dutch state railway.

More groups sold

European state railways were on a roll with such expansions, as Deutsche Bahn, the German counterpart, bought Arriva in August 2010 for £1.5billion, though European competition authorities required it to sell its operations in Germany (to the Italian state railway). Arriva was delisted from the stock exchange.

Two of the other UK-owned PLCs followed suit in 2022. Stagecoach rejected a takeover by National Express and was sold to German investment fund DWS, while Go-Ahead was acquired by a consortium of Australian transport group Kinetic and Spanish infrastructure company Globalvia; Kinetic has the larger holding.

Kelsian, the parent of Transit Systems following its merger with fellow Australian group Sealink (Kelsian is an anagram of Sealink), was losing interest in its London arm, which had lost out in tendering rounds. It disposed of Westbourne Park garage (the last part of what it had acquired of CentreWest) to a new joint venture with RATP called RATP Dev Transit London in which it retained a 12.5% shareholding in the enlarged business. That was in December 2021.

That left Lea Interchange which it sold to Stagecoach in June 2022. Stagecoach acquired HCT Group's London bus operations two months later.

So where does that leave the ten red bus companies sold 30 years ago? German-owned Arriva and Stagecoach each encompass two of those companies, Singapore-owned Metroline has two and a large part of a third, French-owned RATP has a majority shareholding in one and a small part of a second, while Go-Ahead — owned by a Spanish/Australian consortium — owns the other two.

There is one significant player in British ownership, however, as in 2023 Abellio sold its English bus and rail business to a management buyout called Transport UK Group. It has no direct connection with the businesses sold in 1994/95, but it operates out of former London Transport garages at Walworth in south-east London and Fulwell in the south-west, so the Union Flag still flies figuratively over those parts of the old empire. ■

Tootbus is RATP's new trading name — Toot is short for The Original Open Tour — for the London sightseeing business that it acquired from Arriva in 2014. DLP262 (LJ51 DKO) is a Plaxton President-bodied DAF DB250 that began life is a closed top vehicle with Arriva London. ALAN MILLAR

East Yorkshire's
independent years

JOHN WHITEING shows some of the great variety of vehicles that the company operated over the 31 years between its sale by the National Bus Company and acquisition by Go-Ahead Group

The roots of East Yorkshire go back to the end of 1919 when Ernest John Lee purchased a Ford Model T bus to operate a service between Elloughton and Hull; in 1922 a Mr Beaulah was taken into partnership forming Lee & Beaulah. Two years later Hull & District Motor Services was set up by HA Harvey to run a service between Kirk Ella and Hull.

The British Automobile Traction Company (BAT) — part of British Electric Traction (BET) — registered the name East Yorkshire Motor Services (EYMS) on October 5, 1926 in order to take over these two operators, whose vehicles provided

Parked alongside Hull Paragon railway station in August 1987 is Daimler Fleetline 872 (RAT 872G), the last of seven new in 1969 with Park Royal bodywork to the modified Beverley Bar profile. It survives in preservation. This site was formerly occupied by the corporation's central bus garage which was destroyed in the Blitz of May 7/8, 1941 with the loss of 44 motorbuses, with a further 21 damaged. After clearance, the resultant hard standing became known as The Muck to generations of bus employees and survived for around 50 years before being redeveloped as Hull Interchange and the St Stephen's Shopping Centre.

EYMS's initial fleet; it adopted Lee & Beaulah's dark blue and primrose as its livery.

Four more local operators were taken over later that month as part of a consolidation of bus services within the city of Kingston upon Hull and the East Riding of Yorkshire. Its services eventually operated as far beyond the East Riding as Leeds (jointly with the West Yorkshire Road Car Company), Selby and Goole (both in the West Riding, if only just) as sole operations and to Scarborough in the North Riding in co-operation with, but not jointly with the United Automobile Company.

A coordination agreement was concluded with Kingston upon Hull Corporation in July 1934 regarding operations within the city and the immediately surrounding area; this held, with slight amendments, until the early 1980s. Upon the dissolution of the Tilling & BAT bus group in 1942, EYMS passed back to BET.

The East Riding was, and remains today, a predominantly rural area with only the city of Hull and the towns of Beverley and Bridlington offering any significant urban settlement. The town services in Beverley were operated by the local company Cherry's Coaches and thus denied to EYMS, while coastal Bridlington was subject to seasonal variations.

The operations of EYMS were further complicated by the need for specially designed and unique double-deck bodywork for routes which passed through the medieval gothic arch of the North Bar in Beverley and by a requirement for lowbridge double-deckers for the routes to Goole and Selby and also by some routes to Hornsea until the bridges were either rebuilt or, in the case of Hornsea, demolished subsequent to the closure of the railway.

Traditional lowbridge buses could not pass comfortably through the Beverley Bar and the original designs of buses for the Bar could not pass beneath the low bridges. Things changed with the advent of the AEC Bridgemaster (EYMS having the country's largest fleet of this model) and, later, the AEC Renown and Daimler Fleetline whose lower floor provided the opportunity to design a modified (and far less distinctive) roof profile which satisfied both restrictions.

EYMS was subsumed into the National Bus Company (NBC) in 1969, and lost its traditional indigo livery for corporate poppy red and white, although initially buses were painted indigo in NBC-style, EYMS being one of only a tiny number of subsidiaries to use anything other than leaf green or poppy red.

Privatisation and deregulation

As a precursor to the breaking up of NBC, United's operations from Scarborough and Pickering depots, comprising 70 vehicles, were transferred to EYMS in 1985. This made geographic sense as the area involved had always had much more in common with the East and West Ridings than with the heartlands of United's operations in north-east England from which they were separated by the North Yorkshire Moors. Thus, EYMS gained a further significant area of urban operations, albeit with some seasonal variation.

EYMS became independent in February 1987 following a management buyout and remained so until June 2018 when it was acquired by the Go-Ahead Group, thus becoming the last but one

Arriving at Hull Coach Station (as the 1935-built bus station was known) in August 1987 was highbridge Alexander-bodied Daimler Fleetline 889 (WKH 889J), one of ten new in 1971, the first double-deckers delivered following the diversion of services along the newly-constructed relief road in Beverley, thus avoiding the need to operate through the North Bar. It retained NBC poppy red and white livery but with the newly-introduced East Yorkshire fleetname on its lower front dash.

former NBC bus-operating subsidiary to join one of the major groups.

While traditionally EYMS had run the out-of-town services and Kingston upon Hull City Transport (KHCT) the local ones, following deregulation in October 1986 there was a

Awaiting departure to Ampleforth from Valley Bridge bus station in Scarborough in August 1987 was 112 (PRA 12R), a former East Midland Leyland Leopard with Alexander T-type bodywork, one of six new in 1976. All passed to United in 1984, with the last five spending many years allocated to Scarborough, until East Yorkshire acquired them with the operations there.

considerable increase in EYMS's operations within the city boundaries, in order to consolidate its position. This resulted in significant competition, not just between these two incumbent operators, but new ones such as Citilink, Metro City Bus and Rhodes. Over time, EYMS acquired many of the competing operators including Metro City Bus and Rhodes, while KHCT bought Citilink and expanded it to become its low-cost operation. EYMS also acquired Cherry's Coaches in 1987, turning it into its coaching and touring subsidiary.

This expansion led to an incredible variety of buses joining EYMS , both from acquired operators and many other sources across the nation. ◾

These two contemporary but contrasting single-deckers in Beverley depot in August 1988 were acquired two months earlier with the business of Phillips, Shiptonthorpe but never operated with East Yorkshire. SKB 685G was a Park Royal-bodied Bristol RELL6G new to Liverpool Corporation (the only buyer for that chassis/body combination) and LCB 55G was a Leyland Tiger Cub with East Lancs bodywork new to Blackburn. EYMS operated Phillips for a year as a subsidiary and then absorbed it into the Cherry's Coaches business.

Leyland National 170 (MOD 819P), new to Western National in 1976 and parked on The Muck in August 1988 with the roof of Paragon railway station towering behind, was one of many Leyland Nationals acquired in the early years of competitive operations in Hull. Alongside is Park Royal-bodied Leyland Atlantean AN68/1R 905 (RCN 112N), new to Gateshead & District in 1974 and acquired from Northern General.

One of several vintage vehicles acquired by East Yorkshire, in this case from PK Historic Omnibus of Hunmanby, was open-top East Lancs-bodied Leyland Titan PD2/37 602 (202 YTE), new to Lancaster City Transport in 1963 and converted to open-top by Lancaster in 1977. When photographed at Corner Café terminus in Scarborough in September 1989, it retained its white and blue Lancaster livery. It was repainted later in East Yorkshire colours.

Park Royal-bodied Daimler Fleetline GOG 591N, new to West Midlands PTE in 1975, was acquired when Revill Bus of Langtoft, near Driffield, ceased operating its competitive service between Beverley and Hull, with odd journeys to Driffield. It became 891 in the Scarborough & District fleet for use on a service to Warners Holiday Village at Cayton Bay and was photographed at Valley Bridge bus station in Scarborough in August 1990. The fixed destination display had only recently been applied.

ABOVE: *East Yorkshire acquired seven AEC/Park Royal Routemasters from London Buses in 1988 to compete with KHCT in Hull, and by 1994 had 19 from a variety of sources, all painted in pre-NBC indigo and primrose. Loading in Beverley bus station in August 1990 was 812 (ALM 65B), one of three sourced in 1989 from Road Car which had acquired them with the takeover the previous year of Gash, Newark. It was operating on the half-hourly 121 service to Hull, conductor operation enabling a 25min journey time, 8min faster than one-person operation. It was later converted to open-top for operation in Scarborough.*

LEFT: *A September 1990 view of 16-year-old Park Royal-bodied Leyland Atlantean AN68/1R 952 (TIJ 952), originally registered PAT 952M. It was extensively refurbished at the end of 1989 and re-registered shortly afterwards as a prototype for the mooted treatment of all of this batch of 15, but it remained unique. Little of the exterior was changed apart from the addition of an Alexander R-type front dash and fitting a digital destination display, EYMS's first use of this technology.*

Former Hardwick's 1981 Leyland Leopard 236 (PNW 336W) was rebodied with East Lancs EL2000 dual-purpose bodywork in 1992, having originally been a Plaxton Supreme coach, and shortly afterwards was re-registered DDZ 236. It was in Pickering town centre in July 1995, en route from Helmsley to Scarborough, on service 128 which was a combination of the former United route of the same number and the erstwhile Hardwick's service from Scarborough to Ebberston.

East Yorkshire acquired four long-wheelbase Leyland Olympians with ECW's coach bodywork from London Country North East in 1988. These included 543, which had been new to London Country for the 757 Luton FlightLine service as LRC7 (B107 LPH). East Yorkshire gave 543 the registration B111 WAT from a Leyland Tiger coach. It was operating service 746 from York to Hull when photographed in Beverley bus station painted in standard bus livery but with the addition of a red flash on the roof coves.

Eastbourne
1980 revisited

MIKE GREENWOOD had a photo feature published in Buses Annual 1984 which was titled A Day in the Life. This captured the buses of Eastbourne Borough Council taken on one particular day, July 11, 1980

Forty years ago in 1984, most of the pages in that year's *Buses Annual* were printed in black and white, with just eight of the 128 pages, plus the front cover, incorporating colour photographs.

Forty years on, I thought it would be rather nice to revisit the photos I took in Eastbourne in July 1980 but this time to add an injection of colour. Unfortunately, I did not take enough colour photos on the day in question, so this time around, I have used those I took over the period either side from July 7 to 12 that year. ∎

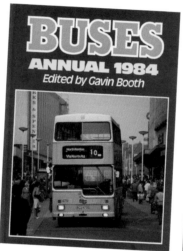

A Day in the Life

MIKE GREENWOOD looks at Eastbourne Borough Council buses on July 11, 1980.

The weather had brightened up by Friday 11 July when these two Leyland Atlanteans were photographed in Terminus Road with the attractive railway station building and its splendid clock tower, built in 1886, as a backdrop. A third Atlantean can just be seen heading out of town in the far distance. The leading Atlantean is 32 (YJK 932V), a 33ft AN68A/2R which was one of four added to the fleet in August and September 1979. All have bodywork by East Lancs. Eastbourne was such a loyal customer of the Blackburn-based bodybuilder that in July 1980 the entire fleet had East Lancs bodywork.

This busy scene in Terminus Road was captured on July 7. A 1961 AEC Regent V, 57 (HJK 157), sneaks between 73 (BJK 673D), a 1966 Leyland Titan PD2A/30, which is heading in the other direction and 31 (VDY 531T), a 1978 Leyland Atlantean AN68A/2R.

Photographers seem less keen to take pictures of the rear of buses, yet these can be helpful to preservationists, transport historians and modellers. This is Regent 57, new in June 1961 but entered before delivery into the Blackburn Carnival by East Lancs and awarded first prize in its group. The Regent Vs were in the twilight of their lives with only five left in the fleet by July 1980 and used only on peak hour workings. The Alliance Building Society became the Alliance & Leicester in October 1985.

ABOVE: *Eastbourne's bus garage in Churchdale Road dated back to July 1905. When visited on July 11 there were eight buses inside, five Leyland Titan PD2A/30s and three AEC Regent Vs. Also present, on the left-hand side parked nearest to the camera, was the tow-bus, numbered 98, operating on trade plate 230 HC. This was 1963 Regent V 66 (KHC 366), converted following withdrawal in May 1975.*

LEFT: *This rear view of Leyland Titan PD2A/30 80 (BJK 680D), the last of ten delivered in March and April 1966, shows the comprehensive rear destination blind and the curious indented offside corner panel with three chrome strip guards. Directly in front of it is one of Eastbourne's 13 single-deckers in 1980, a Leyland Panther.*

Open-top Leyland Titan PD2A/30 84 (DHC 784E) passing a Renault 16 car and the Glastonbury Hotel on the Royal Parade as it makes the journey to the foot of Beachy Head via the sea front. New in June 1967, 84 had the top of its roof removed in June 1973. In 1979 it was named Seafront Sunbus but from ground level it was still difficult to tell that it was actually an open-topper. This may explain the lack of passengers on board upstairs, although the absence of sunshine may have been another factor. It was not until May 1985 that the upper-deck side windows were removed and replaced with handrails.

LEFT: *Leyland Titan PD2A/30 81 (DHC 781E) was one of five 60-seaters which arrived in June 1967. It was photographed at the junction of Cornfield Road and Lushington Road while operating a service 4H working to the General Hospital.*

BELOW: *The other major operator in Eastbourne was Southdown. Here we have 3211 (411 DCD), a 69-seat Northern Counties convertible open-top bodied Leyland Titan PD3/4 'Queen Mary' which was new in May 1964 and originally numbered 411. It was making its way along the Grand Parade with Eastbourne's open-top PD2A/30 No. 84 following. Between the two buses can be seen the domed roof of the elegant pier building which was destroyed by fire in July 2014. The Southdown Titan is carrying a good load of passengers on service 197 to Birling Gap, part of the Seven Sisters chalk cliffs, one of the longest stretches of undeveloped coastline on the south coast. The route ran via Beachy Head. Eastbourne service 6A, on which 84 is operating, ran to the foot of Beachy Head via the sea front.*

The last of the final batch of five AEC Regent Vs, delivered in May 1963, was 70 (KHC 370) which waits on Marine Parade for its next duty on the Town Tour. It was a regular performer on this service and accordingly had platform doors fitted in October 1970.

The green giant

In 12 years, Flixbus has grown from three intercity coach routes in southern Germany into a global giant with a presence across three continents, and is expanding rapidly in Britain

Flixbus is a child of the deregulation of scheduled coach services in its native Germany and other western European countries.

Founded in Munich in 2011 by three tech entrepreneurs, it has worked with partner operators to grow from an initial three routes in Bavaria to become market leader in Germany and to establish services across Europe, North and South America.

It adopted its green livery in 2015 when it merged with German rival Meinfernbus, shortly before expanding into France, the Netherlands, Scandinavia, central and eastern Europe and Turkey. It acquired Stagecoach's European operation of Megabus services in 2016 and having already launched its own branded services in the United States in 2018, its parent company Flix bought the iconic Greyhound Lines from FirstGroup in October 2021. Flix also operates Flixtrain-branded rail services in Germany.

Flixbus wants to become Britain's biggest express coach operator by 2025. It began operating coach services in in England in July 2020 and although the Covid pandemic suppressed demand for several months, it has since grown with several English, Scottish and Welsh partners to provide a rapidly expanding network of services to rival those of the longer established National Express and Megabus. A protracted dispute between Britain's train operators and rail unions in 2022 and 2023, with a succession of strikes, has helped increase demand for coach travel. ∎

The blue roof and air conditioning pod on this Higer-bodied Scania K410EB6 Touring at the railway station in the French city of Dijon in April 2018 is a clue that it was previously 55119 in Stagecoach's Megabus fleet in France, one of 28 similar coaches delivered in 2015 and acquired by Flixbus in 2016. Dijon-based partner operator Autocars Linck was operating it on a service to Lyon. ALAN MILLAR

An MAN Lion's City of Flixbus partner Held-Reisen at the central bus station in Hamburg in April 2017, departing on a journey of around 150miles south to its home city of Hess Oldendorf. Orange has since been dropped from the livery. ALAN MILLAR

Departing for Birmingham from Victoria Coach Station in London in June 2023, with two National Express Caetano Levantes and an Adventure Travel coach working for Megabus in close pursuit, was YN72 ZRC, a Scania K410EB6 with Irizar i6S body in the fleet of Birmingham operator Bouden Coach Travel. ALAN MILLAR

In Birmingham in August 2022 on a London-Glasgow service via Manchester was brand new 0613 (SJ22 HBA) in McGill's Loch Lomond Bus Service fleet, a Volvo 9700 integral. RUSSELL YOUNG

Nottingham-based Tiger European is the operator of TY69 GER, a 57-seat Mercedes-Benz Tourismo M/3, waiting to take up a journey from London Victoria. ALAN MILLAR

Showbus
The first 50 years

TONY WILSON pays photographic homage to what grew quickly into Britain's biggest annual rally for preserved and modern buses and coaches

On a winter's day in January 1973 I attended what turned out to be a fledgling bus rally that led to the first 50 years of Showbus. Held within the grounds of Brunel University at Uxbridge in west London, student Martin Isles had organised a gathering of buses as part of the university's annual Brunelzebub event.

Martin went on to become Dr Martin Isles, a schoolteacher, but back then he chaired the university's Bus Society and had been persuaded that this would be an interesting addition to the festivities. Thus was spawned what grew into Showbus, a summer event first as part of the Middlesex Show in Hillingdon where it stayed until 1979. Sponsorship aided its growth through the likes of the Pickfords removals company and later National Express.

In 1979, Grey-Green took over the sponsorship and having outgrown the annual showground's event, moved to Thorpe Park in Surrey in 1980. The following year, 1981, the plan was to hold it at Brockwell Park in south London as part of the Lambeth Show, but the Brixton riots put paid to that. Help was at hand when Ensignbus stepped in and hosted it on its premises at Purfleet in Essex.

Then came 11 years at Woburn Park in Bedfordshire from 1982 to 1992, when Lord and Lady Tavistock threw open their gates to Showbus.

That was not without its problems as the good old British weather did not help at times. The combination of soft wet grassland and heavy buses and coaches was not a good mix. Tractors were employed on occasions to extricate vehicles sunk to their axles. But it was not all bad as the sun did shine on the event, sometimes.

With diecast model maker EFE Gilbow its new sponsor, it moved again in 1993 to the much harder standing of the Imperial War Museum at Duxford in Cambridgeshire, an airfield with good drainage. By now, Showbus had grown to entrants in the 100s and was turned into Showbus International, with operators and manufacturers willing to showcase their vehicles from home and abroad.

Duxford — like Woburn, it is close to a motorway junction — remained its home until 2013 when it left the southern part of the country for Middle England at Long Marston in Warwickshire. It returned to Duxford in September 2014 but only for the one year before making one last visit to Woburn in 2015, an event remembered more for the weather-related ground conditions than the entrants.

It was in the East Midlands from 2016 to 2018 at Donington Park, once again a site with good hard standing and no soft ground issues, before revisiting its southern roots with a new home at the

One of the most colourful vehicles to attend Brunelzebus in January 1973 was Eastern National 2385 (WNO 481), an Eastern Coach Works-bodied a Bristol KSW open-topper entered by local coach operator Valliant-Silverline and used to promote the European tour of Paul McCartney's Wings pop group. It was restored to this condition in time for the 2023 Showbus Flyby.

At Hillingdon Showground in 1975 was this splendidly preserved 1931 AEC Regal with Burlingham bodywork in the livery of original owner Morley's Provincial Garage of Leicester as its R1 (JF 2378).

Hertfordshire Showground near Redbourn. Covid meant a change of plan for September 2020, with Showbus Flyby, a spectator event with vehicles running along the A40 between the outskirts of Oxford and Beaconsfield. Showbus proper returned to the showground in 2021, albeit on a smaller scale.

There was another change of plan in 2022, the 50th year of Showbus if we count Brunelzebus (which we should). Dr Isles intended to bow out of the event with two consecutive weekends of Showbus activity, first another Flyby and then back to a showground display on the second weekend. The showground event ran as planned September 26, but the Flyby was postponed for a year as it was scheduled for the day before the funeral of Queen Elizabeth II.

However, holding the Flyby in June 2023 ensured that Showbus reached its 50th anniversary and that, whatever happens to the event in the future, the many enthusiasts who trekked to the various locations around England had an opportunity to recognise all that Martin Isles and his many able assistants have done to entertain us since 1973. ∎

One of the longest vehicles to be entered for Showbus when it was held within the parkland grounds of Woburn Abbey was South Yorkshire PTE 2009 (FHE 292V) in 1982, a Leyland-DAB bendybus with Leyland National body new two years earlier for a free service in Sheffield city centre.

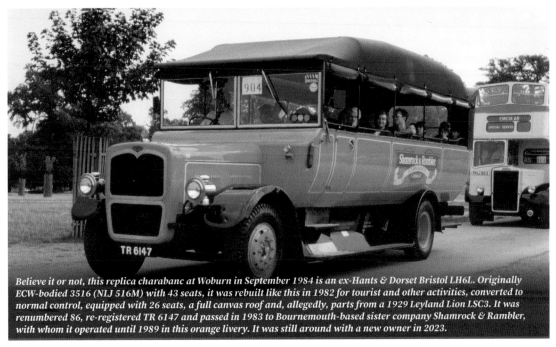

Believe it or not, this replica charabanc at Woburn in September 1984 is an ex-Hants & Dorset Bristol LH6L. Originally ECW-bodied 3516 (NLJ 516M) with 43 seats, it was rebuilt like this in 1982 for tourist and other activities, converted to normal control, equipped with 26 seats, a full canvas roof and, allegedly, parts from a 1929 Leyland Lion LSC3. It was renumbered 86, re-registered TR 6147 and passed in 1983 to Bournemouth-based sister company Shamrock & Rambler, with whom it operated until 1989 in this orange livery. It was still around with a new owner in 2023.

West Riding 803 (JHL 983), one of three AEC Reliances with centre-entrance Roe Dalesman coach bodies new in 1957 for private hires and express services, leading three cars through the Woburn parkland towards the rally site in 1992.

Strachans-bodied Sunderland Corporation 53 (FBR 53D), a 1966 Leyland Panther, at Woburn in 1992. Sunshine highlights the livery and transatlantic styling of its two-door body with trapezoid windows, a design unique to the Wearside city.

Carters of Ipswich brought this seriously adjusted Bristol VRT to Duxford in 2008. New to Ribble in 1977 as standard ECW-bodied double-decker 2009 (CBV 9S), it had moved on to Milton Keynes City Bus when, in 1993, it suffered major damage to the upper deck and was set to be scrapped. However, the Guide Friday sightseeing company bought it and had it rebuilt as a single-decker, named **Prudence** *and re-registered to HNP 165S for its Cotswold Tour.*

Themed displays became a hallmark of Showbus, and this line-up at Duxford in 2011 was of ECW-bodied Bristol single-deckers. From left to right, these are Crosville SC4LK SC13 (783 EFM) from 1957, Eastern National MW5G 480 (217 MHK) from 1959, Bristol Omnibus Company MW5Gs 2933 (923 AHY) from 1959 and G2522 (357 MHU) from 1961, North Western RELL6L 382 (SJA 382K) from 1971, Hants & Dorset 1971 RELL6G 3048 (UEL 564J) from 1971 and Colchester Corporation RELL6L 24 (SWC 24K) from 1972.

Living up to the International part of the Showbus name at Long Marston in 2013 was this preserved 43-seat General Motors PD-4501 Scenicruiser from the iconic Greyhound fleet in the United States. It was new in 1954 and is resident in England. Quite some beast and certainly turned many heads.

Making a splash at Donington Park in 2017 was the display team of heritage coaches from Johnson Bros of Worksop. In the lead was former W Gash of Newark GAL 967, a 1944 Bedford OWB with 1952 Duple Vista body, with behind and to the right Bedford VAL14 5188 RU with Plaxton Panorama body new in 1963 to Excelsior of Bournemouth. The trio was completed by LHE 601W, a 1981 Volvo B58 with Plaxton Supreme body.

At the Hertfordshire Showground in 2022 were two contrasting Southend Transport double-deckers from the Ensignbus heritage fleet, 23 years of age apart. Van-Hool Astromega TD824 coach 245 (JEV 245Y) was one of three new in 1983 for the cross-London X1 service to Heathrow Airport. Routemaster 122 (VLT 44), ex-RM44 of 1960, was one of several acquired in the early 1990s for competitive local services.

This selection begins and ends with an ECW-bodied Bristol K, with the sun shining on another 2022 entry, Thames Valley 446 (DBL 154), a 1946 K6A with lowbridge body.

In the **Dark Peak**

JOHN YOUNG ventures into the scenic countryside east of Stockport to explore the varied history of two routes in the 18 years after deregulation

In the regulated era, Greater Manchester Transport 1410 (AJA 410L), one of 25 ECW-bodied Bristol VRTs ordered by North Western Road Car and delivered to Selnec PTE in 1972, on service 363 at Mellor in March 1985. There is a conductor aboard to assist with reversing on the couple of journeys extended beyond the Devonshire Arms to Moor End.

This article focuses on two semi-rural routes that were extensively revised at deregulation in 1986, running between Stockport, New Mills and Hayfield. The 361 ran up the A6 via Disley, while the 363 served Marple, Marple Bridge and Mellor. They joined at New Mills, diverting to serve Thornsett on their way to Hayfield, from where the 361 continued to Glossop.

Some of the more rural of Stockport's routes, those in the Mellor area in particular have long held a fascination for me, as they serve a community that has been in Greater Manchester since 1974, but is situated in the Dark Peak. The village owes its existence to the cotton trade. Samuel Oldknow, a successful businessman, established a mill there during the Industrial Revolution, but this was destroyed by fire in 1892.

In recent decades, Mellor's bus services have had a chequered history and have witnessed a plethora of operators. Today the village is served by rather indirect service 375 which combined several previous routes and is funded by Transport for Greater Manchester. After many years of operation by Stagecoach Manchester, Go Goodwins (trading as Little Gem) won the contract to run the route from April 2021. When Little Gem ceased operations in April 2023, D&G Bus provided a reduced replacement, down from hourly, six days a week to only four buses a day.

The 375 turns at Shiloh Road, half a mile or so beyond Moor End, just at the Derbyshire boundary and almost within sight of New Mills. ∎

For a short period immediately after deregulation in October 1986, Trent set up a base to run some Glossop area services. Vehicles included Leyland National 456 (PRR 456R), at Stockport bus station in February 1987 after running a trip on the 363.

By October 1987, Crosville was running service 363 journeys to Mellor (Moor End) on a Greater Manchester PTE contract, usually with Leyland Nationals like Gardner-repowered SNG404 (KMA 404T). Crosville remained in National Bus Company ownership until March 1988.

East Midland, trading as Frontrunner, was next to operate the 361 and 363, with a network revision which filled the missing link between Mellor (Moor End) and New Mills. Among the variety of vehicles used was 435 (KSA 186P), one of half a dozen ex-Grampian Alexander-bodied Leyland Atlanteans, photographed at Thornsett in June 1989 when bound for Stockport.

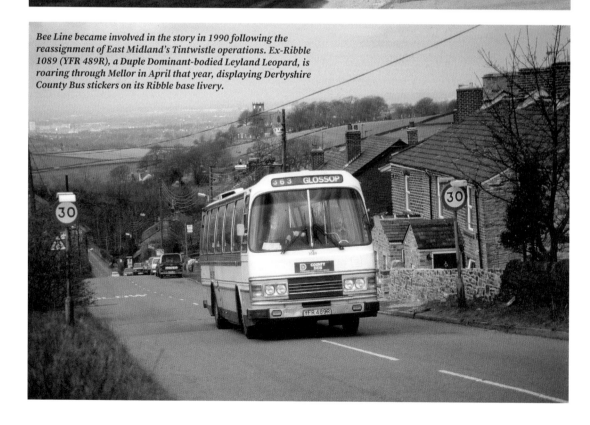

Bee Line became involved in the story in 1990 following the reassignment of East Midland's Tintwistle operations. Ex-Ribble 1089 (YFR 489R), a Duple Dominant-bodied Leyland Leopard, is roaring through Mellor in April that year, displaying Derbyshire County Bus stickers on its Ribble base livery.

Somewhat ironic was the use of an ex GMPTE Leyland Atlantean/Park Royal by Bee Line. Beeline 1645 (XJA 531L), a Park Royal-bodied Atlantean sold as surplus by Greater Manchester Transport, at the main stop in Marple, the Navigation Hotel, in November 1990. Buses in Beeline yellow and red fleet livery were rare on these services.

There then followed a period when GM Buses operated the 361 from its Glossop depot, usually with MCW Metrobuses which accounted for the entire double-deck allocation. A snowy January 2, 1993 sees 5028 (GBU 28V) climbing to Thornsett on its return to its home base.

A newcomer appeared on the scene in the shape of the Glossopdale Bus Company which eventually ran some of the journeys on the 361 on a commercial basis and bought ex-South Yorkshire Reeve Burgess-bodied Dodge S56 minibuses for the purpose. This March 1993 view shows D117 OWG loading in Stockport.

Glossopdale also had some larger vehicles, among the more unusual of which was C203 GKR, a Wright TT-bodied Bedford YMT new to Maidstone Borough in 1986. When photographed passing Birch Vale Post Office in March 1994, it was the largest bus in the fleet.

Stagecoach Manchester acquired the Glossopdale business in 1999 and with it the 361. Glossop depot again ran the service, double-deckers still covering many trips. By then 16 years old, 3124 (B124 TVU), a Northern Counties-bodied Leyland Olympian, was climbing a snow-dusted Chunal Hill in late December 2001 as it made its way from Glossop towards Hayfield.

On the most remote section of the 361, near the Grouse Inn between Glossop and Hayfield, in March 2004 was Stagecoach Manchester 15314 (H464 GVM), a Northern Counties-bodied Scania N113DRB, part of a small batch bought by GM Buses for comparative trials with the Dennis Dominator, Volvo Citybus and Leyland Olympian. Travelling this route on the top deck was a pleasurable experience.

Coach services in the
Emerald Isle

Coach services have expanded across both sides of the border in the island of Ireland, as **MARK BAILEY** was reminded on a visit there in June 2022

A few weeks touring Ireland provided a fascinating insight into the coach network that crisscrosses the island. In the Irish Republic, state-owned Bus Éireann provides countrywide coverage through its Expressway network, while Translink — also state-owned — fulfils a similar role in Northern Ireland using the Goldliner brand delivered by its Ulsterbus operating arm. Both have routes that cross the border. Bus Éireann also operates coaches on commuter services into Dublin and on public service obligation routes in other parts of the country.

Competition in the Republic seems particularly healthy on routes serving Dublin city and Dublin Airport. The following selection of photographs is a snapshot of the variety of operators, liveries and vehicle types to be found. ■

Expressway livery on Bus Éireann SE57 (161 D 16185), an Irizar i6-bodied Scania K410EB6 coach, in Killarney on service 40A from Tralee to Cork. The company has purchased large numbers of Scania coaches with this Spanish coachbuilder's bodies since 2000.

Thirty VDL Futura FHD2-139 integrals joined Bus Éireann's Expressway fleet in 2021, including LX23 (211 D 24266) departing Waterford on service 40 to Cork.

The most recent purchases for Bus Éireann's public service obligation interurban routes are low-entry Sunsundegui SB3-bodied-Volvo B8RLEs with coach seating. Sporting the Transport for Ireland blue livery is VB437 (192 D 24953), arriving in Sligo on cross-border service 458 from Enniskillen to Ballina.

Transport for Ireland's latest green and yellow livery on Bus Éireann LF427 (211 D 35372), a VDL Futura FDD2-130 double-deck coach for Greater Dublin commuter services. It was leaving Busaras, the Dublin city bus station, for Kells, 40miles to the north-west.

For many years the express service linking Dublin and Belfast was a joint operation between Ulsterbus and Bus Éireann, but the latter withdrew from it in December 2020. Ulsterbus 1127 (XUI 2927), a Sunsundegui SC5-bodied tri-axle Volvo B11R, is pictured in Newry on the X1 heading for Belfast.

A subtle marketing change to Translink's express network has led to coaches being refreshed as Goldliner instead of Goldline. Unique to the Ulsterbus fleet is a batch of Caetano Invictus-bodied Scania K410UB6 double-deckers, of which 2040 (WUI 4240) is seen approaching Belfast's Europa Buscentre on the premier service 212 from Derry~Londonderry.

Go-Ahead Ireland was awarded a tranche of Dublin commuter routes serving Co. Kildare and Co. Offaly in 2019, for which 11 VDL Futura SDD130 double-deck coaches were transferred from Bus Éireann and painted in Transport for Ireland blue. This is 31302 (181 D 8449) loading outside Connolly Station on service 120 to Edenderry, spelt Éadan Doire in Irish.

Aircoach was formed in 1999 and acquired by the FirstGroup in 2005. It operates express services linking Dublin Airport and Dublin city with Cork, Galway, Athlone, Belfast and, following the acquisition in January 2023 of the Airporter business, Belfast Airport and Derry~Londonderry. Typical of the fleet is Plaxton Panther-bodied Volvo B11R C49 (201 D 8142), loading in Cork on service 704X to Dublin Airport. Seven coaches based in Belfast for the 705X service have Northern Irish registrations. It also operates commuter routes to communities to the south of Dublin.

ComfortDelGro-owned Irish Citylink, with the same livery as the group's Scottish Citylink, runs services connecting Dublin Airport and Dublin city with Galway, Limerick, Cork and Athlone using coaches provided by Callinan of Claregalway. It also operates service 923 between Galway and the Connemara town of Clifden, on which Van Hool TX16 Alicron integral 151 G 4068 was loading in Galway coach station. The eireagle.com branding was used originally to market the non-stop express routes direct to Dublin Airport.

Cummer Coaches runs GoBus.ie-branded services linking Galway and Cork with Dublin City and Dublin Airport, and one between Galway and Ballina. Awaiting departure from Galway Cathedral on service 430 to Ballina is 171 G 3899, a tri-axle Volvo 9700 with B11R running units. In July 2022 the operation and 31-strong fleet was sold to ComfortDelGro for €12million, and under the new ownership the services are being marketed jointly with those of Irish Citylink and given a new combined livery.

National Express entered the Irish market in March 2020 with Dublin Express, a new service operated on its behalf by Bernard Kavanagh of Urlingford, linking the airport and city centre. Pictured passing the Custom House inbound on service 782 is Mercedes-Benz Tourismo BK10 (161 D 58278), transferred from NatEx's Kent subsidiary The King's Ferry.

Dublin Coach, branding itself as Big Green Bus, has a network of routes serving Dublin, Cork, Waterford, Kilkenny, Limerick, Ennis, Killarney and Tralee. Significant fleet investment in early 2022 added ten new Ayats Horizon-bodied Scania K450EB6 double-deckers, including 221 KE 2313 in Waterford working the 600 service from Cork to Dublin via Kilkenny and the M9 highway.

Metro 3143 (LGZ 5143), a diesel-engined Wright StreetDeck, at Doagh Road, Monkstown on route 2a, the first that Bob Hind sampled in Belfast.

A tale of two cities

Former bus company managing director **BOB HIND** has also been to Ireland, spending two days riding on city buses in Belfast and Dublin, casting a professional eye on how they match the standards that passengers expect

Most local buses in Belfast and Dublin are publicly-owned and that is where the similarity between the two Irish cities ends. A visit to experience both networks is quite revealing so, after an early flight, I am walking from Belfast City Airport (commemorating the city's footballing hero George Best) to find my first Metro bus of the day.

It is Monday morning peak time and, on this trip, I hope I have allowed ample time to get a taste of Belfast's buses. The Metro network is entirely operated by Translink, the government-owned public transport company. The network radiates from the centre on 12 major corridors and, although numbered 1 to 12 (there are two circular routes 13 and 14), the network designers have managed to use a considerable number of the letters of the alphabet for minor route variations or even for different times of day. Consequently I may experience a route 10h later in the day, suggesting at least nine variations to service 10.

Fortunately, my first bus from Sydenham station, inconveniently some distance from the airport, is on time at 07:29 and I am quickly transferred to the city centre. Also fortunately, all the stops are named, numbered and generally carry

Metro 918 (KFZ 9918), a Volvo B7RLE with Wright Eclipse 2 body, in Donegall Square West with a zero-emission Wright StreetDeck Electroliner behind on route 5a. The single-decker on route 6a is headed for Forestside, where Bob Hind caught it to return to the city centre.

timetable information from each stop. And stop announcements are made on board all the buses, so what could go wrong?

The first impression on arriving in Belfast city centre is the Metro fleet has a striking pink livery far more colourful than the drab livery used on the interurban Ulsterbus vehicles. All the Metro routes have stops around or adjacent to City Hall in Donegall Square so finding your bus is not too difficult. Translink produces a schematic map of the network which has a little artistic licence and is not always helpful. There are no hard copies of timetables, everything is online, but at least timetable changes are regulated so advance planning can be done with relative confidence.

Twelve routes

I had decided to test each of the 12 routes, not necessarily in order, but being suburban all are generally between 20 and 30min long and frequencies, particularly into densely populated residential areas, are every 10 to 20min.

Service 2 serves the area north of the city to Monksmoor, alongside the M5. It has ten variations although some are very infrequent peak differences. I am on the 08:00 2c which proves to be a school bus but at least keeps to time. The inbound traffic is often stationary. It is not long before I am reminded of the turbulent history of this city. Huge murals decorate many buildings, some with positive messages: 'Peace cannot be by force, only by understanding' but many still portray raw memories.

At Monksmoor, I return to the centre by 1a, only seven variations to this sub-network. Having climbed gradually away from the city, the slow descent gives panoramic views across Belfast Lough and, as I find throughout the day, the Harland & Wolff shipyard cranes *Samson* and *Goliath* dominate the skyline from most angles.

At Glengormley, we pass the Tramways shopping centre which takes its name from the old (independent) Cavehill & Whitewell Tramway. The line, initially horse and later steam-operated, opened in 1882. Electrified in 1906 and absorbed into the municipal system in 1911, it closed in 1949.

We follow the long, straight Antrim Road back towards the city centre but I leave the bus at Carlisle

Circus not far from the notorious Crumlin Road Gaol. It closed in 1996 and is now a visitor centre. Although the high walls are still symbolic, it is actually an attractive piece of architecture perhaps belying its history.

My next plan was to catch a 12c, northwest towards Carr's Glen and return to the centre by the 11a. I am easily confused; although there should have been a 12min gap between the 12c and 12a, the latter arrives a few minutes before I expect the 12c and I mistakenly board it. This results in a long uphill walk at Ballysillan and a 25min wait for the next 11a.

However, at 10:39 the 11a carries me back to town through Ardoyne along the Shankill Road past a garden of remembrance with a tank as its centrepiece. A more striking and unexpected mural is a dedication to the former Glasgow Rangers manager Walter Smith, 'Heroes get remembered, legends never die'.

I am back in the centre for the 11:10 10h which will be my longest trip, a little circuitously to the south of the network. Again I am slightly confused, this time by the three stops in Queen Street all for

route 10 — the 'h' is the farthest away from City Hall. We leave the city along the Falls Road where the many Gaelic murals attract the tourist buses but are overshadowed, I think, by the beautiful blossoms outside the children's hospital.

At Falls Park depot, we change drivers and the bus continues to climb slowly before turning left near the Donegal Celtic football ground and descends to its terminus at the Black Road park-&-ride site adjacent to the M1. The site has very few cars and the 10h appears to be the only bus serving it only every 30min.

A short walk takes me to Finaghy Crossroads where I expect to catch the 11:56 9a back to town. It catches me unawares at 11:51, the first discrepancy of the morning, but I am happy to travel along Lisburn Road back to the city centre for a short lunch break. As with most of the radial routes, Lisburn Road is a continuous line of local shops and the 9a proves to be a very busy route.

More adventures in Metroland

My afternoon will be spent in the south and west quarters of Metroland, starting with a short experience of service 8. This route has only four

The latest double-deckers for Metro have dual-door bodies, including battery-powered Wright StreetDeck Electroliner 3559 (YUI 2339) waiting to depart the city centre on a 5a to Braniel.

Also in service on the day of Bob Hind's visit to Belfast was Metro 5002 (XUI 8002), a Wright StreetDeck Hydroliner with hydrogen fuel-cell propulsion. PAUL SAVAGE

variants, the shortest of which, the 8d, is a 16min ride to Stranmillis. It proves to be a considerable contrast to the morning's history. We pass Queen's University, very Oxbridge-looking and we are definitely in student land except it is visibly upmarket. The buildings and residences are in an attractive leafy area and even the drinking holes are decidedly posh (from the outside).

I am back at City Hall for the 13:30 7a which runs behind the university but passes many similar annexes. Its ultimate destination is Four Winds and Laurelgrove but I leave it at Forestside, a large out-of-town shopping centre from where the 6a will take me back to the centre, but not before it has travelled around three sides of Forestside. As we approach the centre we get a widescreen view of Greater Belfast lying between the low ranges of hills and Belfast Lough. And always the H&W cranes towering 100m above everything else.

My last combination of routes, outward on the 5a back on the 4e, will take me to a large housing estate at Braniel perched on the side of a hill overlooking this vast panorama. As we near the city centre for the last time we pass a dilapidated shop front with Belfast City Transport Social Club over the frontage. BCT is now in the distant past. In many ways Metro has moved forward in bounds.

The afternoon has been mainly devoid of sectarianism although in Clarawood Estate stand a Union flag and St George's flag in the middle of the community. I have passed a multitude of churches with their own messages outside and every type of political and religious depiction. It is very difficult to ignore Belfast's past.

But its local bus network is something to celebrate. The fleet is generally modern and cleaner than most I have ridden on. The services were mostly punctual and the on- and off-bus information is excellent. The network is a traditional pattern but it works and is well-used. My £6 day ticket was exceptionally good value. I made 15 single journeys which would have cost me £27.

Dublin's spines and radials

Dublin is a contrast. Its population is over 2million and it spreads across a much larger area than Belfast. Despite another traditional looking network, mainly focused on the city centre, Transport for Ireland produced a dynamic Bus Connects plan ('more people to more places more often') in 2020 to create spine routes supplemented by local radials.

Three of these spines and one orbital had already been introduced by the time of my visit (there

Go-Ahead Ireland 12113 (182 D 16107), a Wright StreetLite DF, at Blanchardstown on hourly Dublin route L52 from Adamstown. It is in an earlier Transport for Ireland livery, superseded by the green and yellow of the Go-Ahead and Dublin Bus vehicles behind.

will be eight spines in total and four orbitals) and I aim to try these four routes today. State-owned Dublin Bus is the largest operator in the area, with over 1,000 vehicles carrying more than 140million passengers annually.

I have awoken earlier than expected and, as my first bus terminates outside my hotel, I opt for an early start at 06:40. In most cities the N4 would indicate a night service, but in Dublin this orbital is a 24hr route incredibly running every 10min from 05:30 to 23:30 (every 15min on Sundays) and only dropping to half-hourly for the other 6hr. It begins at The Point, a developing area in the docklands part of the city where the RedLine Luas tram also terminates.

What is even more surprising is how busy, considering the frequency, the service is at this time of morning. Stop announcements are in English and Gaelic, stop information is comprehensive but I find one aspect very frustrating. The online timetables only show departure times at the start of the route and frequencies. There are then estimated running times between a small selection of, seemingly, arbitrary locations. The N4 I am on is shown to have a journey length of 93min but only shows estimated times between six points. I realise

the counter-argument will be high frequency routes do not need timetables, but I am about to prove how wrong that attitude is.

The N4 circles the north of the city through Killester, Donnycarney and Finglas between The Point and Blanchardstown, through very busy residential and industrial areas. Along the way we stop at most stops, the bus is rarely less than half full, yet when we arrive at Blanchardstown it is 07:50. We have completed the full journey in 70min. Furthermore I spend the next 90min in the very modern shopping centre and, at one point, there is a 30min gap in N4 arrivals, presumably caused by peak hour disruptions.

I really dislike the distorted UK timetables that have emerged under the pressure of the traffic commissioners' punctuality rules, but Transport for Ireland has to be more honest with the travelling public who should not have to guess when their next bus is due.

Go-Ahead service

As it happens, my next service, the L52, has a conventional timetable. It is operated by Go-Ahead Ireland and runs hourly between Blanchardstown and Adamstown, although I will only be travelling halfway to Lucan Village. Blanchardstown is a fine example of how the Irish Republic has developed over the past 50 years; how it now has one of the strongest economies in the world. From a small village 10km north-west of Dublin in the 1960s, Blanchardstown is now a sprawling shopping centre housing over 180 big brand stores, cafes and restaurants.

Once we leave this urban centre at 09:20, the L52 is a pleasant relief through semi-rural country lanes across a narrow bridge and a level crossing. I am dropped in the Main Street of a pretty little Lucan Village but there is no indication that my next bus, the C3, serves the same stop. The other thing lacking from the spine network timetables is a specific description of the timing point, on the few occasions there is one. Lucan proves to be slightly bigger than my first impression but I walk towards what appears to be a main road and am relieved to see a C4 crossing the junction.

For 12 years between 1928 and 1940, Lucan was the eastern terminus of Dublin's tram network; now it is connected to the city four times an hour by the combined C3/C4. My C3 appears at 10:03 and

we are soon passing beneath the extensive Liffey Valley Shopping Centre which I will visit later. I am amused to pass the King's Hospital School next to The Dead Man's Inn, serving since 1702.

We travel quickly along the 24hr bus lane on the side of the Chapelizod bypass dual carriageway and soon reach the very busy Heuston railway station on the western fringe of the city centre. From here we travel along the north side of the River Liffey which dissects the city centre. I alight at Bachelors Walk at 10:32, so the estimated 37min journey has actually taken 29min off-peak.

I cross the river, congested on both sides; the bus lanes seem as busy as the other traffic. I am heading westward again on my third spine, the G2 towards Liffey Valley, but this time by a slower route through large residential areas. This route is allocated 48min and, I suspect, it needs every one of them. We pass under the arch of Christ Church Cathedral, dating back to the year 1030, and leave the bustling centre very slowly. The Parish Church of St James proudly claims 'The Camino starts here'. Apparently it has a Camino centre that issues

Another Go-Ahead Ireland vehicle, Wright Gemini 3-bodied Volvo B5TL 11582 (191 D 41384), at Blanchardstown.

One of Dublin Bus's Alexander Dennis Enviro400ER City electric range hybrids, PA226 (221 D 5713), on route G2 at Liffey Valley Shopping Centre.

passports for the famous pilgrimage to Santiago del Compostela in northern Spain, 2,550km away. A long walk.

We travel through densely populated urban roads but manage to reach Liffey Valley in 46min. This time we are in the bus station that stands on a wide open plateau which is the shopping centre. On my day in and around Dublin, I lose count of the number of large out-of-town retail parks I pass.

From here I am with Go-Ahead again for the every-20min route 76 to Tallaght. There should be one at 11:40 then 12:00; mine arrives at 11:40. We retrace the G2 route for a short distance through the housing estates until we head south though Belgard, arriving in Tallaght at 12:29.

The centre of the town is Belgard Square; buses have stops on the periphery and in the centre of the square which is actually a large car park. Across the road from The Square is Tallaght Stadium, home of Shamrock Rovers, the football club that has often represented Ireland in European competitions.

Off to the coast

My next bus, service 75, again Go-Ahead, will take me to the east coast and a famous destination for

past UK ferry travellers. The digital display counts down to the 12:45 departure, then when the time is reached, disappears although there is no sign of the bus. Two of my fellow passengers laden with shopping begin to fret but, at last, it arrives at 12:50.

We set off for Dun Laoghaire around three sides of The Square and into the original Tallaght Village accessed by a bus-only lane. Again, this route links many suburban areas along the southern edge of Dublin. Dundrum, about halfway along the route, that we reach at 13:43, has an impressive Holy Cross Parish Church and an attractive centre.

We reach Dun Laoghaire at 14:21. It claims to have been the home of the world's first suburban railway station and, at one time, the world's largest harbour. All that is in the past; now it has an attractive waterfront and a busy shopping centre.

There are several transport links back to central Dublin, including the Dart electric railway, but I am opting for service 7 which runs every 15min almost following the coastline. Through Blackrock we can see across Dublin Bay to the port; at Booterstown the nature reserve abuts the four-lane highway. The approach to the city centre has embassies and very attractive Georgian housing. It is also very busy.

For the final time on this trip, we cross the River Liffey into O'Connell Street, which is awash with tourists, particularly around the GPO building. Buses and trams interconnect and, as it is approaching peak hour, I search out my third spine, the H2, in Abbey Street Lower.

The route, while initially through the north suburbs, and for a while alongside the N4 where I started my day, is probably the most scenic. We pass the intriguingly-named Bram Stoker Park (the author was born nearby) then head out towards Baldoyle and Portmarnock with coastal views across the Irish Sea. There are even people swimming in the evening sunshine. The H2 terminates in Malahide, 14km north of Dublin. It is a picturesque little town that obviously attracts day trippers and holidaymakers as there are late afternoon queues for my last bus.

The 17:32 Go-Ahead service 102 returns inland towards Dublin Airport every half hour but not before visiting yet another major shopping centre, this time at Swords where, again, there are queues waiting for us. We arrive at the busy airport bus station at 18:15 where my two-day trip of the Irish capitals ends.

Well-served cities

There is little doubt, from my short experience, that both cities are well-served and are probably a good advertisement for government ownership. Both fleets are modern and clean, even later in the day, and generally well-driven despite some poor roads in parts.

On-bus and roadside information is good, every bus had on-bus announcements, but Dublin Bus timetables could be more informative. It was noticeable in both cities that the vast majority of passengers were using multi-journey tickets which are very good value. My Leap Visitor day ticket, which was excellent value, cost €8. I would have spent €23.40 on my nine journeys.

Overall my experience of public transport in Belfast and Dublin was enjoyable and informative. Both have set standards they should be proud of, and that other cities could learn from. Irish buses are leading the way. ∎

The steadily disappearing blue and navy Dublin bus livery on GT17 (12 D 36072), a Wright Eclipse Gemini-bodied Volvo B9TL, in George's Street Upper, Dun Laoghaire.

Leaving the Falls

Former London double-deckers — RTs and Routemasters — were a feature of the Niagara Falls in Canada for more than half a century. **MICHAEL DRYHURST** explains why they got there, why they have left and where they have gone

The last of Double Deck Tours' Cummins-engined RMLs, the former RML2467 numbered 24 in Canada, at Niagara Falls in 2018. KEITH MCGILLIVRAY

Fifty-eight years after they first appeared there, the red double-deckers of Double Deck Tours departed the Canadian side of the Niagara Falls on April 23, 2023, removing both to residents and tourists what had been an integral sight on the local scene.

Double Deck Tours was the brainchild of Norman Watson, an expat Mancunian who commenced business in May 1965 with buses running every 15min from June to September. His initial tour was comprehensive, covering around 30miles to take in all of the major attractions. You could experience either the whole trip straight through or avail of the hop-on/hop-off alternative, of which this must have been one of the first that any sightseeing tour company provided in the world.

Wide Leylands

His first double-deckers were ex-London Transport Leyland Titan 6RTs, the former RTW127/8/48. Most of the 500 RTW class, London's first 8ft wide motorbuses, were exported, principally to the Ceylon Transport Board in today's Sri Lanka, but Double Deck Tours' 1949 trio were the only ones sold to North America.

For what was essentially a sightseeing tour operation, its next three double-deckers —

purchased from Leyland Motors in a dealer capacity in 1966 — were an odd choice, ex-Crosville DKA319/27/37, Bristol K6As with AEC A173 7.7-litre engine and 53-seat Eastern Coach Works lowbridge bodies.

The sunken gangway on the offside of the upper-deck with bench seats to the left provided only minimal headroom and considerably restricted the viewing possibilities. None of its double-deckers were converted for right-hand running or fitted with safety gates on the open platform.

Ex-London Transport highbridge double-deckers remained the favoured choice and next to arrive was Leyland Titan 7RT RTL1315 in October 1967. The first of a dozen AEC Regent III 3RTs arrived in 1970, when RT1300/60, 2210 were shipped in.

There was another unusual purchase, albeit only as a source of spare parts. This was 1950 ex-Glasgow Corporation AEC Regent III A153 (FYS 253) with highbridge Metro-Cammell body. It had been exported in April 1965 to C&C Transportation of Vancouver, British Columbia, but by July 1977 it had been moved 2,700miles east to Hamilton, Ontario, where ultimately it was abandoned as derelict.

Having standardised on the RT family, it was a given that the company would also acquire Routemasters, the first of which arrived at Niagara

Saunders-bodied RT1360 among typically North American vehicles in July 1976.

Falls in October 1983; these were RM1242, 1548, 1651 and ex-Green Line RCL2255, followed in April 1985 by RM1888 and RM1924. All had AEC engines and were purchased direct from London Transport. Various other Routemasters came from British dealers and North American operators between 1988 and 2001 (three of the survivors in 2023 came from Beach Bus Company in Kittyhawk, South Carolina), and Cummins-repowered RML2467, 2501/55 were purchased from the Ensign dealership in 2004. Three Routemasters were converted to partial open-top for the 2019 season.

It also owned a rear-engined double-decker from 2012 to 2016, left-hand-drive ECW-bodied Leyland Olympian ex-demonstrator B757 UHG, which had operated with Brampton Transit in Ontario since January 1989.

End of the road

Norman Watson's family continued to run Double Deck Tours after he died in February 2006, but in November 2018 the business was sold to Absolute Charters in Halifax, Nova Scotia, already the operator of the world's largest fleet of working Routemasters; besides its home city it operates them in Sydney, Nova Scotia and Saint John, New Brunswick.

Like most leisure businesses, Double Deck Tours was hit hard by the Covid pandemic, compelled to suspend operations in 2020. When they resumed, it was on a reduced scale, as social distancing meant that its buses were permitted to carry only ten passengers, which was unsustainable. Despite a brief return to business in July 2022, a lack of visitors saw operations suspended for the rest of that season

One of the original trio of Leyland Titan 6RTs, RTW128, in May 1980.

The ex-Glasgow AEC Regent III with Metro-Cammell body acquired for parts recovery, FYS 253, surrounded by RTs at Niagara Falls in January 1982.

One of the Routemasters converted to open-top was 17, the former RM797, photographed at the Falls in June 2019 with the updated branding introduced by the operator's new owner. The Southend destination blinds show that this was one of the Routemasters operated there in the 1990s. Double Deck Tours acquired it from the Beach Bus Company in Kittyhawk.

The convoy of ten Routemasters leaving Niagara for New Brunswick along the Queen Elizabeth Way, named in 1939 after the then Queen, later Queen Mother. In the lead is fleetnumber 10, the former RM1618, one of three in the final fleet that operated with Greater Manchester Buses in the late 1980s. It was rebuilt in 2011 with a wheelchair lift in the British offside. Immediately behind it is one of the RCLs.

and it was announced the following December that the company would close permanently, and its ten remaining Routemasters would be transferred 1,120miles north to Nova Scotia.

Former RM797, 1102, 1242, 1604/18, 2162/5, RCL2252/5 and RML2467 set off on a five-day marathon, the convoy accompanied by a support vehicle towing a trailer full of spares, and arrived on April 27, 2023 at the facility of Coach Atlantic in Moncton, New Brunswick where they would be prepared for service.

Thus ended one era and another began. ■